TEACHER EDITION

8

Family Life

David Thomas, PhD

General Editor

a Kendall Hunt Company

Cincinnati, Ohio

The Subcommittee on the Catechism, United States Conference of Catholic Bishops, has found this text, copyright 2011, to be in conformity with the *Catechism of the Catholic Church;* it may be used only as supplemental to other basal catechetical texts.

Consultants

Paul Duckro, PhD
Tim Hogan, PsyD
Tom Everson
Fanny Pedraza

RCL Benziger Development Team

James Spurgin
Editor

Tricia Legault
Design

Laura Fremder
Production

Daniel S. Mulhall
National Catechetical Advisor

Jo Rotunno
Director of Catechist and Professional Development

Susan Smith
Director of Project Development

Ed DeStefano
Publisher

Peter M. Esposito
President

NIHIL OBSTAT
Rev. Msgr. Robert Coerver
Censor Librorum

IMPRIMATUR
† Most Reverend Kevin J. Farrell DD
Bishop of Dallas

May 3, 2010

The *Nihil Obstat* and *Imprimatur* are official declarations that the material reviewed is free of doctrinal or moral error. No implication is contained therein that those granting the *Nihil Obstat* and *Imprimatur* agree with the contents, opinions, or statements expressed.

Send all inquiries to:
RCL Benziger
8805 Governor's Hill Drive • Suite 400
Cincinnati, Ohio 45249
Toll Free 877-275-4725
Fax 800-688-8356

Visit us at www.RCLBenziger.com

20658 ISBN 978-0-7829-1508-2 (Student Edition)
20668 ISBN 978-0-7829-1518-1 (Parent Connection)
20688 ISBN 978-0-7829-1538-9 (Teacher Edition)

ACKNOWLEDGMENTS

Excerpts from *Guidelines for Programs to Reduce Child Victimization* provided courtesy of The National Center for Missing and Exploited Children.

Excerpts from the *National Directory for Catechesis* © 2005, United States Conference of Catholic Bishops, Washington, D.C. Excerpts from the *Charter for the Protection of Children and Young People* © 2006, United States Conference of Catholic Bishops, Washington, D.C. Excerpts from the *Catechetical Formation in Chaste Living: Guidelines for Curriculum Design and Publication* © 2008, United States Conference of Catholic Bishops, Washington, D.C. Excerpts from *Sharing Catholic Social Teaching: Challenges and Directions* © 1997, United States Catholic Conference, Inc., Washington, DC. Excerpts from *Human Sexuality: A Catholic Perspective for Education and Lifelong Learning* © 1991, United States Catholic Conference, Inc. Washington, D.C. Excerpts from *Human Life in Our Day* © 1968, United States Conference of Catholic Bishops, Washington, D.C. Excerpts from the *New American Bible with Revised New Testament and Revised Psalms* © 1991, 1986, 1970 Confraternity of Christian Doctrine, Washington, D.C. and are used by permission of the copyright owner. All Rights Reserved. No part of the New American Bible may be reproduced in any form without permission in writing from the copyright owner.

Excerpts from Benedict XVI, Encyclical Letter, *Deus Caritas Est* (25 December 2005). Excerpts from Benedict XVI, Encyclical Letter, *Caritas in Veritate* (29 June 2009). Excerpts from the Congregation for the Doctrine of the Faith, Instruction, *Donum Vitae* (22 February 1987). Excerpts from the Pontifical Council for the Family, *Preparatory Catechesis for the Sixth World Encounter of Families* (18 January 2009). Excerpts from the Pontifical Council for the Family, *The Truth and Meaning of Human Sexuality* (8 December 1995). Excerpts from Second Vatican Council, Pastoral Constitution on the Church in the Modern World, *Gaudium et Spes* (7 December 1965). Excerpts from John Paul II, Apostolic Exhortation, *Familiaris Consortio* (22 November 1981). Excerpts from the English translation of the *Catechism of the Catholic Church* © 1994, 1997, United States Conference of Catholic Bishops. Libreria Editrice Vaticana. Used with permission. All rights reserved.

CONTENTS

Program Overview

Unit 1: God's Gift of Family

Unit 2: God's Gift of Self

Unit 3: God's Gift of Life

Unit 4: God's Gift of Love

Unit 5: God's Gift of Community

Additional Resources

Welcome to RCL Benziger *Family Life!*

A comprehensive moral catechesis for families with children in grades K–8

RCL Benziger *Family Life* offers unparalleled support for Catholic families. This unique series:

- presents skills and virtues for Catholic family living.
- places human sexuality within the context of Catholic family moral living.
- helps families address the complex issues of contemporary life.
- offers in-depth support for child safety education.
- provides solid support for Spanish-speaking families reflecting the unique gifts and challenges of Latino cultures.

Three Key Components for Each Grade Level

Three key components (Student Edition, Teacher Edition and Parent Connection) provide resources for parents, children, religion teachers and catechists to explore, reflect on and decide ways to integrate into their lives each year on five themes in Catholic family living:

- God's Gift of Family
- God's Gift of Self
- God's Gift of Life
- God's Gift of Love
- God's Gift of Community

Student Edition, Parent Connection, Teacher Edition

Additional Resources

Human Reproduction Booklets for Grades 5 and 6

Level A: The Reproductive System and Procreation

Level B: New Life in the Womb and The Miracle of Birth

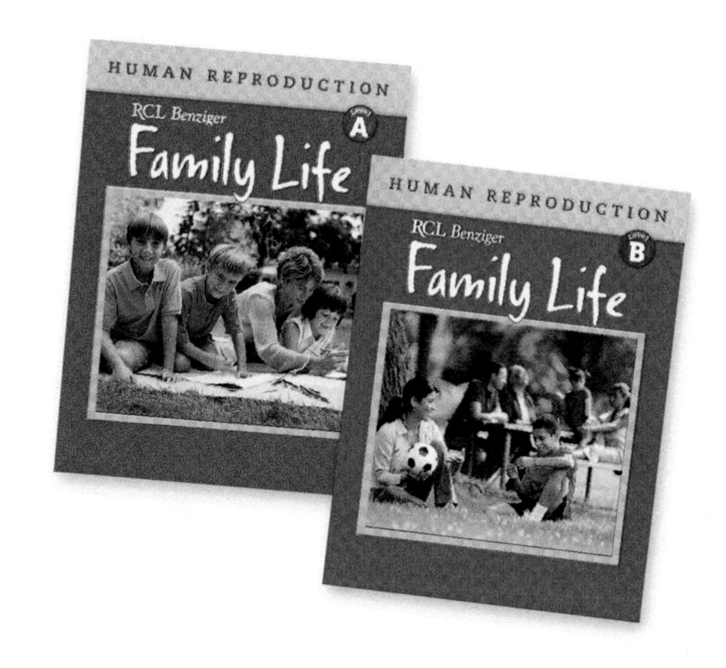

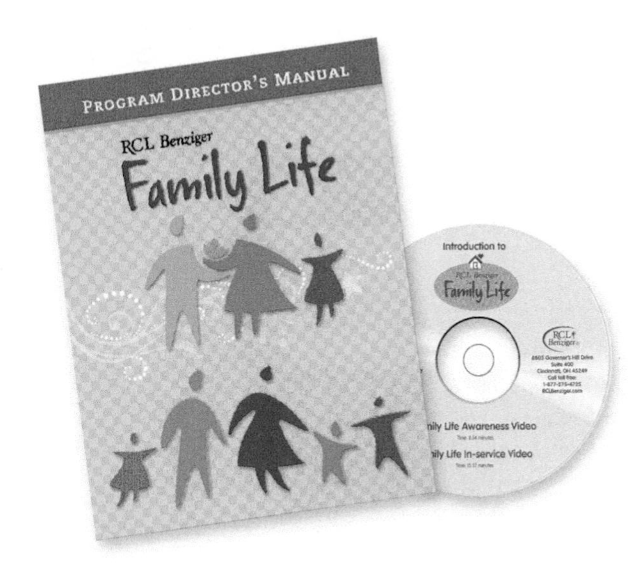

Support for Program Directors

- Program Director's Manual
- DVD in-service video
- Ongoing web support at RCLBFamilyLife.com

In-service DVD

The RCL Benziger *Family Life* DVD contains a video overview of the program and separate in-service segments for teachers, catechists and parents.

Resources for Spanish-speaking Parents

- Parent booklet
- Parent letters for each unit
- Two-page Family Time resource for each unit

Student Edition

RCL Benziger *Family Life* Student Edition guides the child and his or her family through a reflection on each year's curriculum.

Family Time

Each unit begins with a two-page Family Time feature. This feature enables the family and the class to focus on the same themes during the two lessons that make up each unit.

Student Lesson

Each unit includes two lessons. Each lesson has three simple parts: **Engage, Teach,** and **Apply.**

UNIT 1
God's Gift of Family
Family Time

Walking in God's Way

When Jesus was growing up, religion class was time spent with the rabbi in the local synagogue studying God's Word and Law. You might think that Jesus, of all people, wouldn't need to study God's Word and Law. But the Gospels tell us that he followed the rules and fulfilled all of his religious obligations.

Jesus was also obedient to Mary and Joseph. All of his actions and choices reflected the will of God the Father. Those around Jesus misunderstood some of the choices that he made. Some of his choices were even seen as disobedient to God! Jesus' life shows us that sometimes there is a price to pay for being faithful to God's Law.

Jesus lived the virtue of obedience perfectly. In doing so he became a living road map to God's Kingdom: "I am the way and the truth and the life" (John 14:6). Through his teachings as handed down through the Apostles and the Church, Jesus becomes a compass that gives direction to our life. Through both his words and actions, Jesus provides counsel for every aspect of our life. Growing in our relationship with Jesus Christ that began in Baptism is essential to the Christian way of life.

Healthy Habits in the Home

Talk about the Beatitudes (Matthew 5:3–10) as a family. Have each family member choose one of the Beatitudes and list one practical thing they do to live according to that Beatitude. Repeat this exercise throughout the year.

Family Blessings

God our loving Father, continue to bless our family with the Gifts of the Holy Spirit: wisdom, counsel, understanding, courage, knowledge, piety and fear of the Lord. Strengthen us to live our faith in your Son day by day. Amen.

God's Gift of Family 9

he Lesson Home

f each week, have the family sit
le and evaluate the state of the
ness. To encourage each other
ns that will contribute to the
of happiness, develop five simple

p your guidelines for happiness,
ng:

at is our attitude toward one
ow do we show consideration
s of others?

ow do we acknowledge the
each member of our family on

often and how much are we
or share with others in the
we have and who we are?

ow do we speak to one
words and actions? How do
ncourage happiness?

Making Connections

To encourage each member of the family to seek the advice of one another, have family members respond to each of these questions:

- What is happiness?
- What are some ways I can make our home a happier place?
- What are some guiding principles in making moral decisions that support happiness?

on the Fridge

The Holy Spirit is always with us as our Helper. At Baptism we receive the gift of the Holy Spirit. At Confirmation we are strengthened by sevenfold Gifts of the Holy Spirit: wisdom, understanding, right judgment (counsel), courage (fortitude), knowledge, reverence (piety) and wonder and awe (fear of the Lord). These gifts strengthen us to live as faithful disciples of Jesus Christ.

10 God's Gift of Family

Engage: An opening page engages the student, activates their prior knowledge, and grounds the lesson content in the young person's experience.

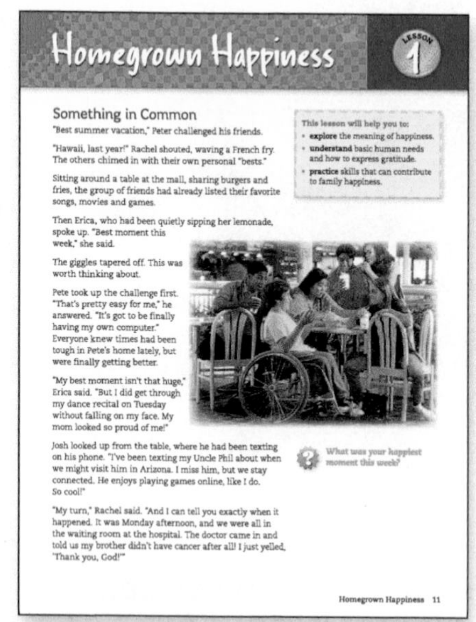

Homegrown Happiness
LESSON 1

Something in Common

"Best summer vacation," Peter challenged his friends.

"Hawaii, last year!" Rachel shouted, waving a French fry. The others chimed in with their own personal "bests."

Sitting around a table at the mall, sharing burgers and fries, the group of friends had already listed their favorite songs, movies and games.

Then Erica, who had been quietly sipping her lemonade, spoke up. "Best moment this week," she said.

The giggles tapered off. This was worth thinking about.

Pete took up the challenge first. "That's pretty easy for me," he answered. "It's got to be finally having my own computer." Everyone knew times had been tough in Pete's home lately, but were finally getting better.

"My best moment isn't that huge," Erica said. "But I did get through my dance recital on Tuesday without falling on my face. My mom looked so proud of me!"

Josh looked up from the table, where he had been texting on his phone. "I've been texting my Uncle Phil about when we might visit him in Arizona. I miss him, but we stay connected. He enjoys playing games online, like I do. So cool!"

"My turn," Rachel said. "And I can tell you exactly when it happened. It was Monday afternoon, and we were all in the waiting room at the hospital. The doctor came in and told us my brother didn't have cancer after all! I just yelled, 'Thank you, God!'"

This lesson will help you to:
- **explore** the meaning of happiness.
- **understand** basic human needs and how to express gratitude.
- **practice** skills that can contribute to family happiness.

What was your happiest moment this week?

Homegrown Happiness 11

Teach: Lesson presentation develops unit theme and highlights vocabulary words

Catholics Believe summarizes the main point of the lesson.

Growing in Virtue highlights the lesson virtue that strengthens the student and family to live a holy and healthy family life.

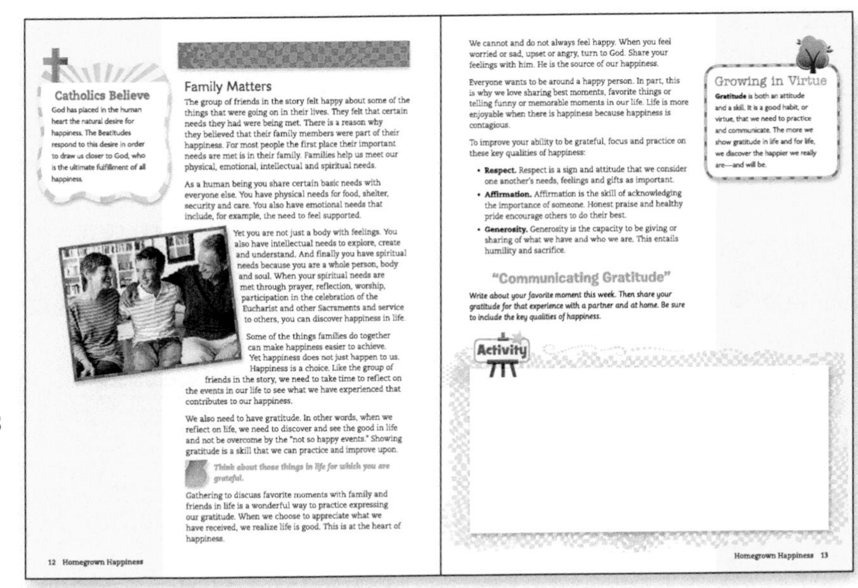

Catholics Believe

God has placed in the human heart the natural desire for happiness. The Beatitudes respond to this desire in order to draw us closer to God, who is the ultimate fulfillment of all happiness.

Family Matters

The group of friends in the story felt happy about some of the things that were going on in their lives. They felt that certain needs they had were being met. There is a reason why they believed that their family members were part of their happiness. For most people the first place their important needs are met is in their family. Families help us meet our physical, emotional, intellectual and spiritual needs.

As a human being you share certain basic needs with everyone else. You have physical needs for food, shelter, security and care. You also have emotional needs that include, for example, the need to feel supported.

Yet you are not just a body with feelings. You also have intellectual needs to explore, create and understand. And finally you have spiritual needs because you are a whole person, body and soul. When your spiritual needs are met through prayer, reflection, worship, participation in the celebration of the Eucharist and other Sacraments and service to others, you can discover happiness in life.

Some of the things families do together can make happiness easier to achieve. Yet happiness does not just happen to us. Happiness is a choice. Like the group of friends in the story, we need to take time to reflect on the events in our life to see what we have experienced that contributes to our happiness.

We also need to have gratitude. In other words, when we reflect on life, we need to discover and see the good in life and not be overcome by the "not so happy events." Showing gratitude is a skill that we can practice and improve upon.

Think about those things in life for which you are grateful.

Gathering to discuss favorite moments with family and friends in life is a wonderful way to practice expressing our gratitude. When we choose to appreciate what we have received, we realize life is good. This is at the heart of happiness.

12 Homegrown Happiness

We cannot and do not always feel happy. When you feel worried or sad, upset or angry, turn to God. Share your feelings with him. He is the source of our happiness.

Everyone wants to be around a happy person. In part, this is why we love sharing best moments, favorite things or telling funny or memorable moments in our life. Life is more enjoyable when there is happiness because happiness is contagious.

To improve your ability to be grateful, focus and practice on these key qualities of happiness:

- **Respect.** Respect is a sign and attitude that we consider one another's needs, feelings and gifts as important.
- **Affirmation.** Affirmation is the skill of acknowledging the importance of someone. Honest praise and healthy pride encourage others to do their best.
- **Generosity.** Generosity is the capacity to be giving or sharing of what we have and who we are. This entails humility and sacrifice.

"Communicating Gratitude"

Write about your favorite moment this week. Then share your gratitude for that experience with a partner and at home. Be sure to include the key qualities of happiness.

Activity

Growing in Virtue

Gratitude is both an attitude and a skill. It is a good habit, or virtue, that we need to practice and communicate. The more we show gratitude in life and for life, we discover the happier we really are—and will be.

Homegrown Happiness 13

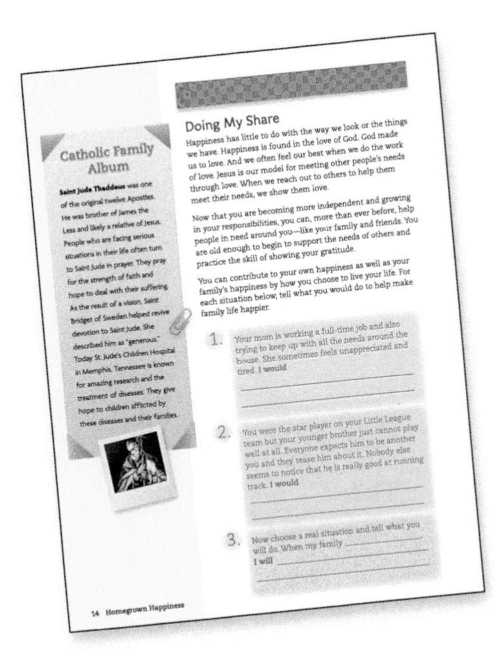

Catholic Family Album

Saint Jude Thaddeus was one of the original twelve Apostles. He was brother of James the Less and likely a relative of Jesus. People who are facing serious situations in their life often turn to Saint Jude in prayer. They pray for the strength of faith and hope to deal with their suffering. As the result of a vision, Saint Bridget of Sweden helped revive devotion to Saint Jude. She described him as "generous." Today St. Jude's Children Hospital in Memphis, Tennessee is known for amazing research and the treatment of diseases. They give hope to children afflicted by these diseases and their families.

Doing My Share

Happiness has little to do with the way we look or the things we have. Happiness is found in the love of God. God made us to love. And we often feel our best when we do the work of love. Jesus is our model for meeting other people's needs through love. When we reach out to others to help them meet their needs, we show them love.

Now that you are becoming more independent and growing in your responsibilities, you can, more than ever before, help people in need around you—like your family and friends. You are old enough to begin to support the needs of others and practice the skill of showing your gratitude.

You can contribute to your own happiness as well as your family's happiness by how you choose to live your life. For each situation below, tell what you would do to help make family life happier.

1. Your mom is working a full-time job and also trying to keep up with all the needs around the house. She sometimes feels unappreciated and tired. **I would** ______
2. You were the star player on your Little League team but your younger brother just cannot play well at all. Everyone expects him to be another you and they tease him about it. Nobody else seems to notice that he is really good at running track. **I would** ______
3. Now choose a real situation and tell what you will do. When my family ______ **I will** ______

14 Homegrown Happiness

Apply: Concluding activity integrates lesson content and invites a faith choice.

Catholic Family Album highlights a Saint or holy person or Catholic organization that exemplifies the lesson theme.

Additional Student Edition Features

- The Catholic Home
  (Includes Catholic prayers and practices)
- Unit reviews
- End-of-the-year review
- Certificate to recognize achievement

Teacher Edition

Your RCL Benziger *Family Life* Teacher Edition offers you comprehensive support including these innovative features:

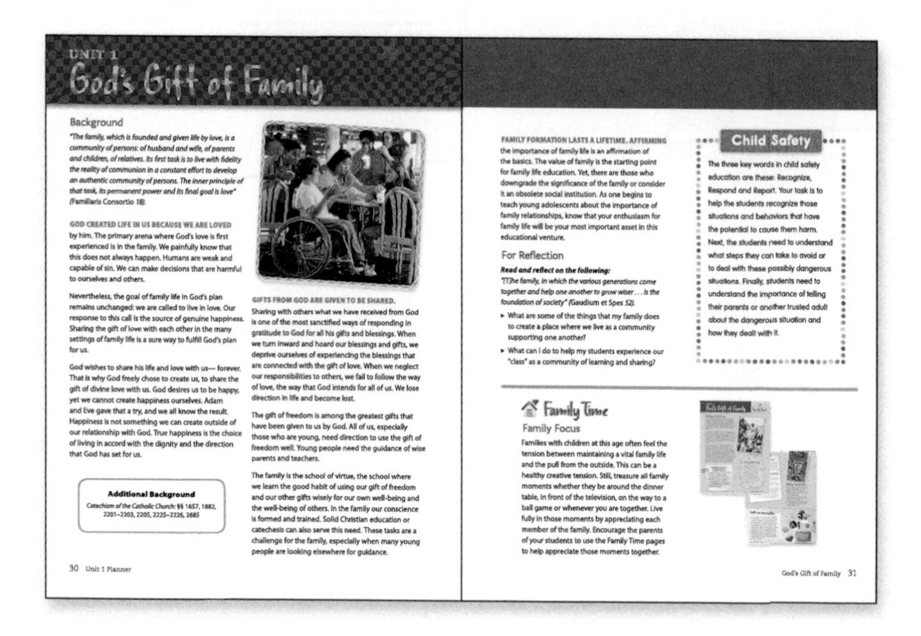

UNIT 1

God's Gift of Family

Background

"The family, which is founded and given life by love, is a community of persons: of husband and wife, of parents and children, of relatives. Its first task is to live with fidelity the reality of communion in a constant effort to develop an authentic community of persons. The inner principle of that task, its permanent power and its final goal is love" (Familiaris Consortio *18*).

GOD CREATED LIFE IN US BECAUSE WE ARE LOVED by him. The primary arena where God's love is first experienced is in the family. We painfully know that this does not always happen. Humans are weak and capable of sin. We can make decisions that are harmful to ourselves and others.

Nevertheless, the goal of family life in God's plan remains unchanged: we are called to live in love. Our response to this call is the source of genuine happiness. Sharing the gift of love with each other in the many settings of family life is a sure way to fulfill God's plan for us.

God wishes to share his life and love with us— forever. That is why God freely chose to create us, to share the gift of divine love with us. God desires us to be happy, yet we cannot create happiness ourselves. Adam and Eve gave that a try, and we all know the result. Happiness is not something we can create outside of our relationship with God. True happiness is the choice of living in accord with the dignity and the direction that God has set for us.

Additional Background

Catechism of the Catholic Church: §§ 1657, 1882, 2201–2203, 2205, 2225–2226, 2685

GIFTS FROM GOD ARE GIVEN TO BE SHARED. Sharing with others what we have received from God is one of the most sanctified ways of responding in gratitude to God for all his gifts and blessings. When we turn inward and hoard our blessings and gifts, we deprive ourselves of experiencing the blessings that are connected with the gift of love. When we neglect our responsibilities to others, we fail to follow the way of love, the way that God intends for all of us. We lose direction in life and become lost.

The gift of freedom is among the greatest gifts that have been given to us by God. All of us, especially those who are young, need direction to use the gift of freedom well. Young people need the guidance of wise parents and teachers.

The family is the school of virtue, the school where we learn the good habit of using our gift of freedom and our other gifts wisely for our own well-being and the well-being of others. In the family our conscience is formed and trained. Solid Christian education or catechesis can also serve this need. These tasks are a challenge for the family, especially when many young people are looking elsewhere for guidance.

30 Unit 1 Planner

FAMILY FORMATION LASTS A LIFETIME. AFFIRMING the importance of family life is an affirmation of the basics. The value of family is the starting point for family life education. Yet, there are those who downgrade the significance of the family or consider it an obsolete social institution. As one begins to teach young adolescents about the importance of family relationships, know that your enthusiasm for family life will be your most important asset in this educational venture.

For Reflection

Read and reflect on the following:

"[T]he family, in which the various generations come together and help one another to grow wiser . . . is the foundation of society" (Gaudium et Spes *52*).

- What are some of the things that my family does to create a place where we live as a community supporting one another?
- What can I do to help my students experience our "class" as a community of learning and sharing?

Child Safety

The three key words in child safety education are these: Recognize, Respond and Report. Your task is to help the students recognize those situations and behaviors that have the potential to cause them harm. Next, the students need to understand what steps they can take to avoid or to deal with these possibly dangerous situations. Finally, students need to understand the importance of telling their parents or another trusted adult about the dangerous situation and how they dealt with it.

Family Time

Family Focus

Families with children at this age often feel the tension between maintaining a vital family life and the pull from the outside. This can be a healthy creative tension. Still, treasure all family moments whether they be around the dinner table, in front of the television, on the way to a ball game or whenever you are together. Live fully in those moments by appreciating each member of the family. Encourage the parents of your students to use the Family Time pages to help appreciate those moments together.

God's Gift of Family 31

Unit Background Pages

A theological and catechetical background essay puts you at ease.

Lesson Planner

A practical lesson planner for each of the ten lessons forecasts everything you will need.

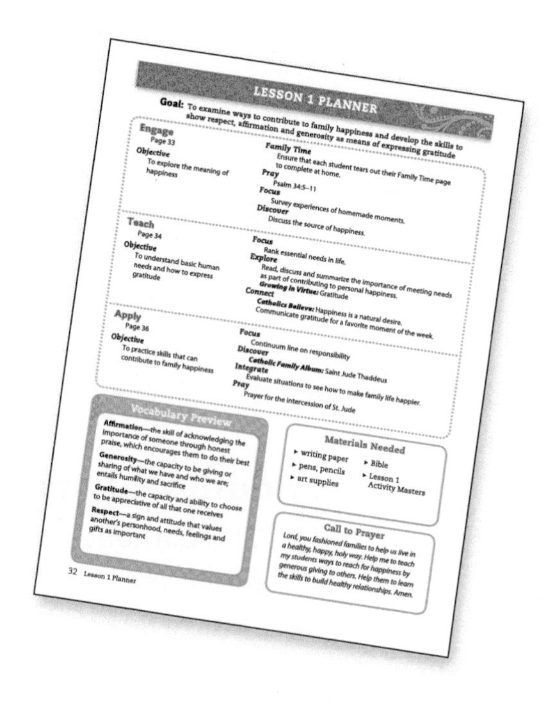

LESSON 1 PLANNER

Goal: To examine ways to contribute to family happiness and develop the skills to show respect, affirmation and generosity as means of expressing gratitude

Engage
Page 33
Objective
To explore the meaning of happiness

Family Time
Ensure that each student tears out their Family Time page to complete at home.
Pray
Psalm 34:5–11
Focus
Survey experiences of homemade moments.
Discover
Discuss the source of happiness.

Teach
Page 34
Objective
To understand basic human needs and how to express gratitude

Focus
Rank essential needs in life.
Explore
Read, discuss and summarize the importance of meeting needs as part of contributing to personal happiness.
Growing in Virtue: Gratitude
Connect
Catholics Believe: Happiness is a natural desire.
Communicate gratitude for a favorite moment of the week.

Apply
Page 36
Objective
To practice skills that can contribute to family happiness

Focus
Continuum line on responsibility
Discover
Catholic Family Album: Saint Jude Thaddeus
Integrate
Evaluate situations to see how to make family life happier.
Pray
Prayer for the intercession of St. Jude

Vocabulary Preview

Affirmation—the skill of acknowledging the importance of someone through honest praise, which encourages them to do their best

Generosity—the capacity to be giving or sharing of what we have and who we are; entails humility and sacrifice

Gratitude—the capacity and ability to choose to be appreciative of all that one receives

Respect—a sign and attitude that values another's personhood, needs, feelings and gifts as important

Materials Needed

- writing paper
- pens, pencils
- art supplies
- Bible
- Lesson 1 Activity Masters

Call to Prayer

Lord, you fashioned families to help us live in a healthy, happy, holy way. Help me to teach my students ways to reach for happiness by generous giving to others. Help them to learn the skills to build healthy relationships. Amen.

32 Lesson 1 Planner

Wraparound Lesson Plans

Creative lesson plans offer you a simple core plan plus teaching tips and ideas for enriching the lessons.

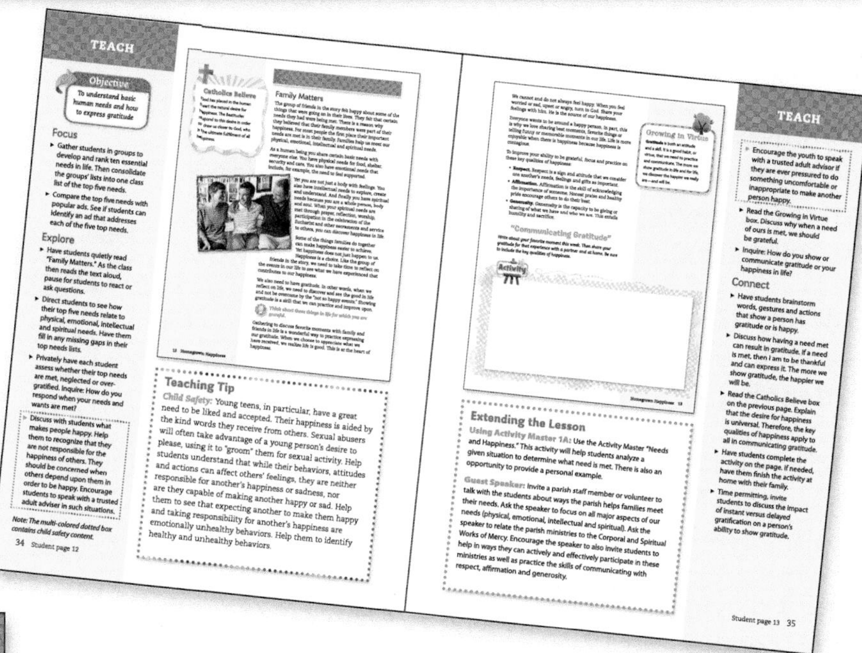

TEACH

Objective

To understand basic human needs and how to express gratitude

Focus

- Gather students in groups to develop and rank ten essential needs in life. Then consolidate the groups' lists into one class list of the top five needs.
- Compare the top five needs with popular ads. See if students can identify an ad that addresses each of the five top needs.

Explore

- Have students quietly read "Family Matters." As the class then reads the text aloud, pause for students to react or ask questions.
- Direct students to see how their top five needs relate to physical, emotional, intellectual and spiritual needs. Have them fill in any missing gaps in their top needs lists.
- Privately have each student assess whether their top needs are met, neglected or over-gratified. Inquire: How do you respond when your needs and wants are met?
- Discuss with students what makes people happy. Help them to recognize that they are not responsible for the happiness of others. They should be concerned when others depend upon them in order to be happy. Encourage students to speak with a trusted adult adviser in such situations.

Note: The multi-colored dotted box contains child safety content.

34 Student page 12

Teaching Tip

Child Safety: Young teens, in particular, have a great need to be liked and accepted. Their happiness is aided by the kind words they receive from others. Sexual abusers will often take advantage of a young person's desire to please, using it to "groom" them for sexual activity. Help students understand that while their behaviors, attitudes and actions can affect others' feelings, they are neither responsible for another's happiness or sadness, nor are they capable of making another happy or sad. Help them to see that expecting another to make them happy and taking responsibility for another's happiness are emotionally unhealthy behaviors. Help them to identify healthy and unhealthy behaviors.

Extending the Lesson

Using Activity Master 1A: Use the Activity Master "Needs and Happiness." This activity will help students analyze a given situation to determine what need is met. There is also an opportunity to provide a personal example.

Guest Speaker: Invite a parish staff member or volunteer to talk with the students about ways the parish helps families meet their needs. Ask the speaker to focus on all major aspects of our needs (physical, emotional, intellectual and spiritual). Ask the speaker to relate the parish ministries to the Corporal and Spiritual Works of Mercy. Encourage the speaker to also invite students to help in ways they can actively and effectively participate in these ministries as well as practice the skills of communicating with respect, affirmation and generosity.

TEACH

- Encourage the youth to speak with a trusted adult advisor if they are ever pressured to do something uncomfortable or inappropriate to make another person happy.
- Read the Growing in Virtue box. Discuss why when a need of ours is met, we should be grateful.
- Inquire: How do you show or communicate gratitude or your happiness in life?

Connect

- Have students brainstorm words, gestures and actions that show a person has gratitude or is happy.
- Discuss how having a need met can result in gratitude. If a need is met, then I am to be thankful and can express it. The more we show gratitude, the happier we will be.
- Read the Catholics Believe box on the previous page. Explain that the desire for happiness is universal. Therefore, the key qualities of happiness apply to all in communicating gratitude.
- Have students complete the activity on the page. If needed, have them finish the activity at home with their family.
- Time permitting, invite students to discuss the impact of instant versus delayed gratification on a person's ability to show gratitude.

Student page 13 35

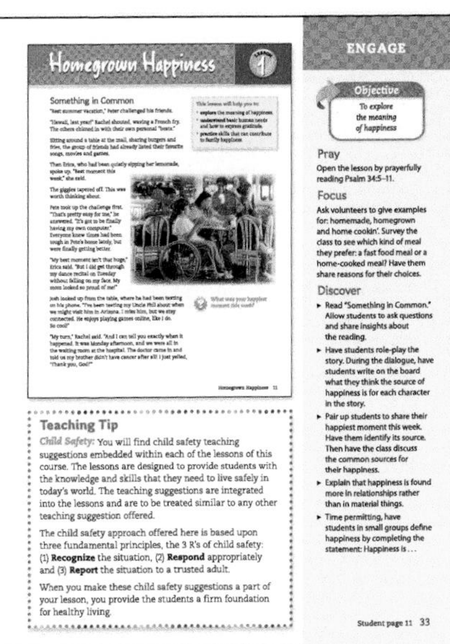

Homegrown Happiness 1

ENGAGE

Objective

To explore the meaning of happiness

Pray

Open the lesson by prayerfully reading Psalm 34:5–11.

Focus

Ask volunteers to give examples for: homemade, homegrown and home cookin'. Survey the class to see which kind of meal they prefer: a fast food meal or a home-cooked meal? Have them share reasons for their choices.

Discover

- Read "Something in Common." Allow students to ask questions and share insights about the reading.
- Have students role-play the story. During the dialogue, have students write on the board what they think the source of happiness is for each character in the story.
- Pair up students to share their happiest moment this week. Have them identify its source. Then have the class discuss the common sources for their happiness.
- Explain that happiness is found more in relationships rather than in material things.
- Time permitting, have students in small groups define happiness by completing the statement: Happiness is . . .

Teaching Tip

Child Safety: You will find child safety teaching suggestions embedded within each of the lessons of this course. The lessons are designed to provide students with the knowledge and skills that they need to live safely in today's world. The teaching suggestions are integrated into the lessons and are to be treated similar to any other teaching suggestion offered.

The child safety approach offered here is based upon three fundamental principles, the 3 R's of child safety: (1) **Recognize** the situation, (2) **Respond** appropriately and (3) **Report** the situation to a trusted adult.

When you make these child safety suggestions a part of your lesson, you provide the students a firm foundation for healthy living.

Student page 11 33

Child Safety

The program integrates key concepts of child safety education across the nine grade levels, kindergarten through grade 8.

- A child safety unit preview is included on the background page.
- Content related to child safety education is highlighted within the lesson plans.

Activities, Reviews and Glossary

Additional resources are available, such as a cumulative glossary of family life vocabulary words found in the back of your Teacher Edition.

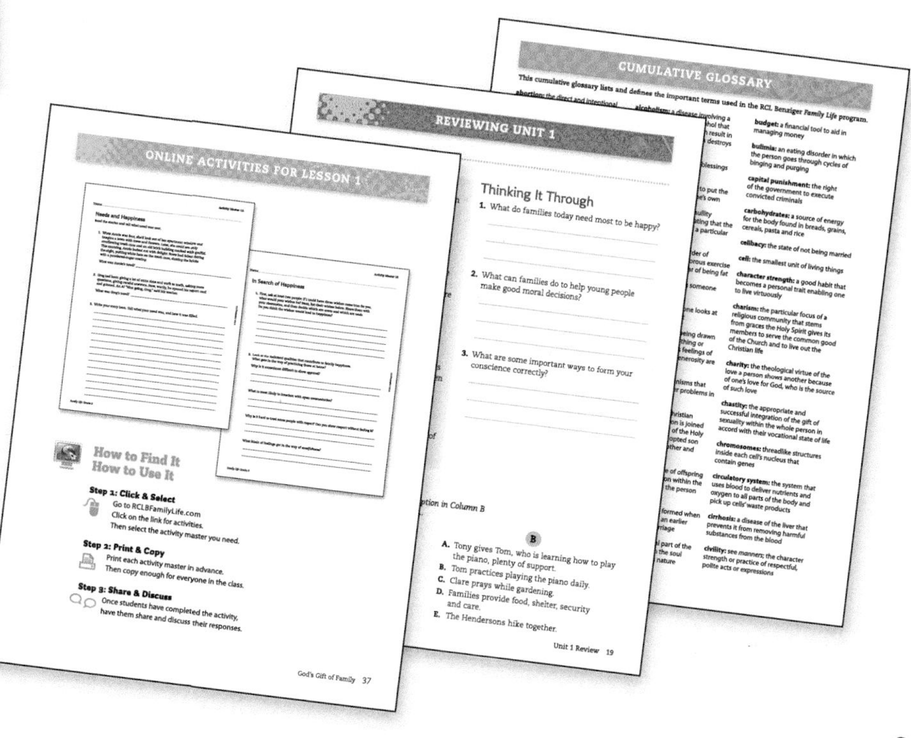

ONLINE ACTIVITIES FOR LESSON 1

How to Find It
How to Use It

Step 1: Click & Select
Go to RCLBFamilyLife.com
Click on the link for activities.
Then select the activity master you need.

Step 2: Print & Copy
Print each activity master in advance.
Then copy enough for everyone in the class.

Step 3: Share & Discuss
Once students have completed the activity, have them share and discuss their responses.

God's Gift of Family 37

REVIEWING UNIT 1

Thinking It Through

1. What do families today need most to be happy?
2. What can families do to help young people make good moral decisions?
3. What are some important ways to form your conscience correctly?

B

A. Tony gives Tom, who is learning how to play the piano, plenty of support.
B. Tom practices playing the piano daily.
C. Clare prays while gardening.
D. Families provide food, shelter, security and care.
E. The Hendersons hike together.

Unit 1 Review 19

CUMULATIVE GLOSSARY

budget: a financial tool to aid in managing money

bulimia: an eating disorder in which the person goes through cycles of binging and purging

capital punishment: the right of the government to execute convicted criminals

carbohydrates: a source of energy for the body found in breads, grains, cereals, pasta and rice

celibacy: the state of not being married

cell: the smallest unit of living things

character strength: a good habit that becomes a personal trait enabling one to live virtuously

charism: the particular focus of a religious community that stems from graces the Holy Spirit gives its members to serve the common good of the Church and to live out the Christian life

charity: the theological virtue of the love a person shows another because of one's love for God, who is the source of such love

chastity: the appropriate and successful integration of the gift of sexuality within the whole person in accord with their vocational state of life

chromosomes: threadlike structures inside each cell's nucleus that contain genes

circulatory system: the system that uses blood to deliver nutrients and oxygen to all parts of the body and pick up cells' waste products

cirrhosis: a disease of the liver that prevents it from removing harmful substances from the blood

civility: see manners; the character strength or practice of respectful, polite acts or expressions

Parent Connection

The Parent Connection magazine supports the parents' role as the first and primary educators of their children in faith and moral living. The magazine provides:

- a moral catechesis for family living related to the lesson themes in the student book.
- practical strategies for communicating and working together as a household of faith.
- tips for discussing difficult issues with young people.
- a glossary of terms taught in the program, according to grade level.

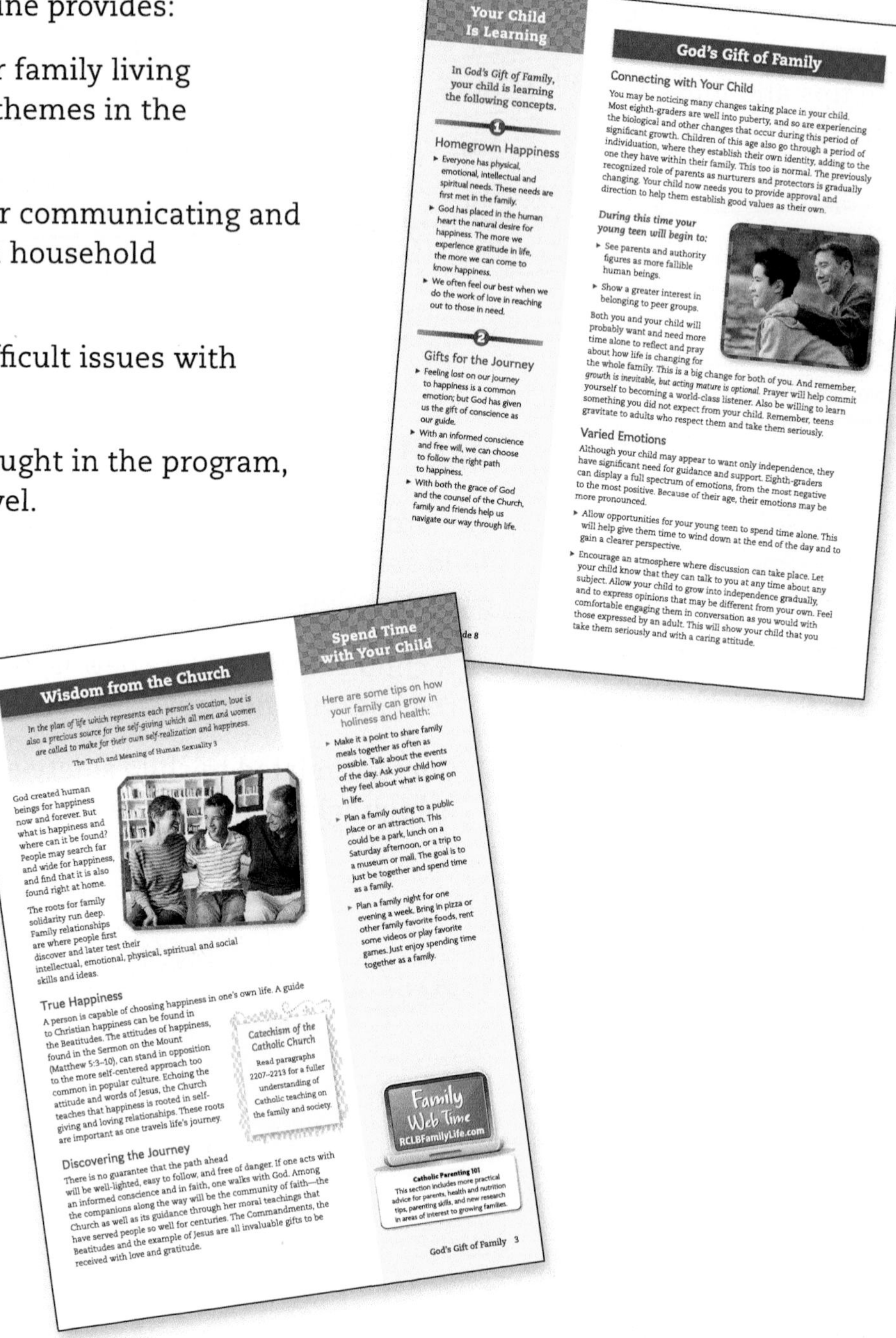

Your Child Is Learning

In *God's Gift of Family*, your child is learning the following concepts.

1

Homegrown Happiness

- Everyone has physical, emotional, intellectual and spiritual needs. These needs are first met in the family.
- God has placed in the human heart the natural desire for happiness. The more we experience gratitude in life, the more we can come to know happiness.
- We often feel our best when we do the work of love in reaching out to those in need.

2

Gifts for the Journey

- Feeling lost on our journey to happiness is a common emotion; but God has given us the gift of conscience as our guide.
- With an informed conscience and free will, we can choose to follow the right path to happiness.
- With both the grace of God and the counsel of the Church, family and friends help us navigate our way through life.

God's Gift of Family

Connecting with Your Child

You may be noticing many changes taking place in your child. Most eighth-graders are well into puberty, and so are experiencing the biological and other changes that occur during this period of significant growth. Children of this age also go through a period of individuation, where they establish their own identity, adding to the one they have within their family. This too is normal. The previously recognized role of parents as nurturers and protectors is gradually changing. Your child now needs you to provide approval and direction to help them establish good values as their own.

During this time your young teen will begin to:

- See parents and authority figures as more fallible human beings.
- Show a greater interest in belonging to peer groups.

Both you and your child will probably want and need more time alone to reflect and pray about how life is changing for the whole family. This is a big change for both of you. And remember, *growth is inevitable, but acting mature is optional.* Prayer will help commit yourself to becoming a world-class listener. Also be willing to learn something you did not expect from your child. Remember, teens gravitate to adults who respect them and take them seriously.

Varied Emotions

Although your child may appear to want only independence, they have significant need for guidance and support. Eighth-graders can display a full spectrum of emotions, from the most negative to the most positive. Because of their age, their emotions may be more pronounced.

- Allow opportunities for your young teen to spend time alone. This will help give them time to wind down at the end of the day and to gain a clearer perspective.
- Encourage an atmosphere where discussion can take place. Let your child know that they can talk to you at any time about any subject. Allow your child to grow into independence gradually, and to express opinions that may be different from your own. Feel comfortable engaging them in conversation as you would with those expressed by an adult. This will show your child that you take them seriously and with a caring attitude.

Wisdom from the Church

In the plan of life which represents each person's vocation, love is also a precious source for the self-giving which all men and women are called to make for their own self-realization and happiness.

The Truth and Meaning of Human Sexuality 3

God created human beings for happiness now and forever. But what is happiness and where can it be found? People may search far and wide for happiness, and find that it is also found right at home.

The roots for family solidarity run deep. Family relationships are where people first discover and later test their intellectual, emotional, physical, spiritual and social skills and ideas.

True Happiness

A person is capable of choosing happiness in one's own life. A guide to Christian happiness can be found in the Beatitudes. The attitudes of happiness, found in the Sermon on the Mount (Matthew 5:3–10), can stand in opposition to the more self-centered approach too common in popular culture. Echoing the attitude and words of Jesus, the Church teaches that happiness is rooted in self-giving and loving relationships. These roots are important as one travels life's journey.

Catechism of the Catholic Church

Read paragraphs 2207–2213 for a fuller understanding of Catholic teaching on the family and society.

Discovering the Journey

There is no guarantee that the path ahead will be well-lighted, easy to follow, and free of danger. If one acts with an informed conscience and in faith, one walks with God. Among the companions along the way will be the community of faith—the Church as well as its guidance through her moral teachings that have served people so well for centuries. The Commandments, the Beatitudes and the example of Jesus are all invaluable gifts to be received with love and gratitude.

Spend Time with Your Child

Here are some tips on how your family can grow in holiness and health:

- Make it a point to share family meals together as often as possible. Talk about the events of the day. Ask your child how they feel about what is going on in life.
- Plan a family outing to a public place or an attraction. This could be a park, lunch on a Saturday afternoon, or a trip to a museum or mall. The goal is to just be together and spend time as a family.
- Plan a family night for one evening a week. Bring in pizza or other family favorite foods, rent some videos or play favorite games. Just enjoy spending time together as a family.

Family Web Time
RCLBFamilyLife.com

Catholic Parenting 101
This section includes more practical advice for parents, health and nutrition tips, parenting skills, and new research in areas of interest to growing families.

God's Gift of Family 3

Additional Components

RCL Benziger *Family Life* offers comprehensive support for the program coordinator.

Program Director's Manual

This comprehensive manual offers a wealth of features to support the program coordinator, teachers, catechists, and parents. All pages are reproducible. Highlights include:

- overview of program
- models for in-service sessions for parents and teachers/catechists
- handouts for in-service sessions
- professional articles
- English and Spanish versions of parent letters
- Spanish translations of all Family Time pages
- scope and sequence chart for entire program
- glossary of key terms and themes
- index of key issues taught throughout the program

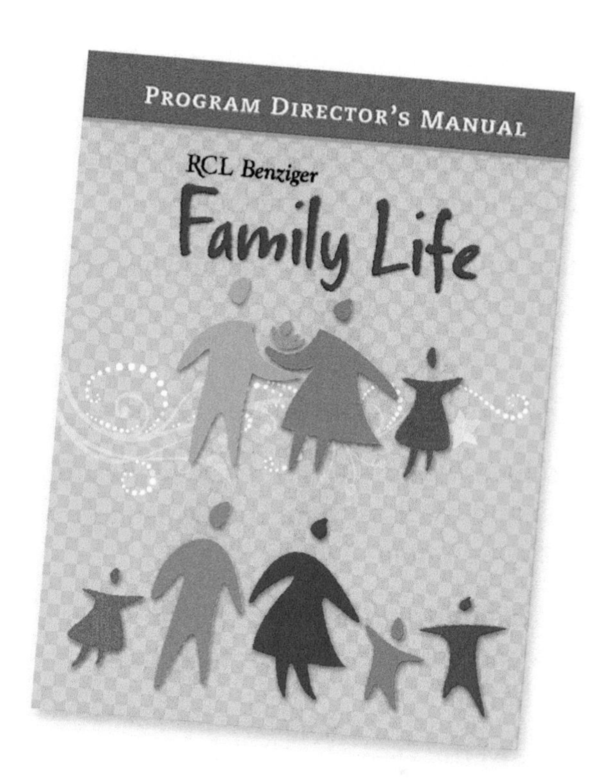

QuickStart Workshop

A practical video-assisted workshop prepares you for your role in family life education.

RCL *Benziger*

Family Life

Web Site

Web support for the program includes a variety of resources for program coordinators, teachers, catechists, students, and parents.

QuickStart for Teachers and Catechists

Introduction

From its inception, RCL Benziger *Family Life* has remained faithful to the enduring vision of assisting the family through resources that help it grow as the domestic Church. RCL Benziger *Family Life:*

- provides a moral catechesis for children from kindergarten to grade eight.
- places human sexuality within the context of Christian moral living.
- offers a catechesis of hope against the challenges facing the Catholic family.
- introduces children to the joys of virtuous living and teaches them the skills to grow healthy and holy.
- teaches children the skills they need to make good decisions to protect them from harm.
- adapts to the changing times and needs of the Church with each new edition.

RCL Benziger *Family Life* is designed to prepare young people to live safe and healthy, moral and loving lives as members of the Christian family. The series provides a catechesis for moral living focusing at each grade level on the five themes of:

- God's Gift of Family
- God's Gift of Self
- God's Gift of Life
- God's Gift of Love
- God's of Community

Why a New Edition of RCL Benziger *Family Life*?

In 2002 the U.S. Conference of Catholic Bishops approved the groundbreaking *Charter for the Protection of Children*. In the Charter the bishops committed the Catholic Church in the United States to "creating a safe environment within the Church for children and youth" (Preamble).

In Article 12 of the Charter, the bishops commit the Church in the United States to "maintain 'safe environment' programs" in accord with Catholic moral principles conducted cooperatively with parents to provide education and training for children.

This edition of RCL Benziger *Family Life* has been revised to assist parishes and dioceses to provide this safe environment training to the Church's children and youth, and to provide support to their parents and teachers who are responsible for their education and safety. RCL Benziger *Family Life* has been revised in consultation with the USCCB Secretariat for Child and Youth Protection, building upon the child safety guidelines developed by numerous (arch) dioceses, and fully incorporating the USCCB 2007 document *Catechetical Formation in Chaste Living: Guidelines for Curriculum Design and Publication*.

The student and teacher materials in the RCL Benziger *Family Life* series have been reviewed by the USCCB Subcommittee on the Catechism and have been found to be in conformity with the *Catechism of the Catholic Church*, and so are deemed to be in accord with Catholic moral principles.

Organizational Structure

There are five units in each book corresponding to the five themes. There are two lessons in every unit. Each lesson is designed to be used in a 45-minute setting, with additional activities suggested to expand the lesson for longer class periods. Each lesson begins and ends with prayer. Suggestions are offered for those who wish to teach two lessons in one class period.

Each lesson flows through three steps: (1) Engage, which activates the child's knowledge of the lesson theme and helps relate the theme to experience; (2) Teach, where the concepts are taught and students begin to connect them to concrete situations; and (3) Apply, where students begin to integrate what they have learned into daily living and make a concrete faith choice.

Each lesson introduces students to a moral virtue related to family and community living, and helps them begin to practice the skills required to live that virtue and make it a personal habit.

Teaching Tips

RCL Benziger *Family Life* strives to teach children skills for living. Skills are learned by practice. Have students use role-play, games, and other interactive methods to practice these skills.

This series addresses many sensitive topics. Many children live in families with only one parent, split-time living between a divorced mother and father, and/or live with a stepparent or guardian. Help students understand that every family is different and that every family has problems. Help students to take pride in their families as they are and not to feel ashamed that they are not perfect. Remind them from time to time that God loves all families.

Enjoy your time discussing the topics in RCL Benziger *Family Life* with your students. Let them know that the topics are serious, but do not suggest by word or deed that the topics are inappropriate or something to fear. Help the students to understand that all the themes that they are learning about are part of everyday living.

Child Safety Education

You do not need to be an expert in child safety to teach this course. You simply have to care about your students and want the best for them. RCL Benziger *Family Life* integrates child safety education into the regular flow of its lessons. Child safety skills are included in every lesson of every grade level. Your role here as a teacher is essential. Learning the skills for moral living and personal safety will last the children for a lifetime and help them to shape their lives.

Here are some suggestions to help you effectively present the materials:

- During this course of study students will learn to distinguish between appropriate and inappropriate touches. According to child safety experts, adults need not be afraid to touch children appropriately. For example, pats on the back and shoulder squeezes are okay. If a child wishes to hug you, accept the gesture, but maintain control of the hug (e.g. length, tightness) in a subtle way.
- While children are encouraged to express their feelings, they will sometimes reveal in public more than is appropriate. If you feel that the sharing gets too personal and is inappropriate, stop and thank the child for sharing. If you suspect that abuse may have occurred, speak to the child privately after class.
- Students will be taught what to do if they feel they have been touched inappropriately. If a child reports inappropriate touching to you, you have an obligation to report it. Every state and local community has its own established procedures to follow when reporting child abuse. Be familiar with those for your local area and follow them carefully. Also report the incident to the person in charge at your parish or school.
- As the teacher you must be prepared if a student reports inappropriate touching or another form of abuse. If a child reports they are being abused to you:
  - — Give thanks to God that the child feels safe enough with you to share this burden.
  - — Be prepared to let the child talk for as long as they need.
  - — Avoid asking questions; do not interview or interrogate; but do take notes, if possible, so that you can report accurately what the child says.
  - — Respect the child's privacy; do not discuss the situation with the child in public or anywhere that others may overhear. Consider what you have been told as privileged information that should only be shared with the proper authorities.
  - — Affirm the child's feelings; help them to see that they are doing the proper thing; let the child know that it is okay to feel frightened or afraid, sad and even relieved.
  - — Be honest about what will happen next ("I have to report what you told me to the police. They will want to talk with you. I will stay with you until . . .").
  - — Thank the child for speaking to you; let the child know how brave they are for speaking up.

Family Life Resources to Use with the Family

Each unit of RCL Benziger *Family Life* provides components to support the partnership between the teacher/catechist and the family.

Parent Connection

One of the most important resources is the Parent Connection magazine, which comes with each student text. The Parent Connection component informs the parents on what their child is learning, and instructs parents to help their child apply what has been learned. It also includes parenting tips for raising a Catholic family and suggestions of how to respond to children's questions concerning human sexuality. These grade level specific magazines are available only in English.

Hablando de la sexualidad con mis hijos is an informative and colorful 32-page booklet written for Spanish-reading parents. It offers background material on the five unit themes and assists parents in speaking about sexuality issues with their child of various ages. In addition, it addresses specific issues in Latino family life.

Student Edition

Core Lessons: The ten core lessons of each grade level student book explore, develop, and apply the moral teachings of the Catholic Church as they relate to the daily life of the Christian family. Parents may teach these lessons at home or enlist the help of their parish or school. Every lesson relies on parental involvement to be successful.

Family Time: Two Family Time pages open each unit of every student book. Written to the parents, these take-home pages inform the parents of the content to be studied in the coming lessons in the unit, focus on the spiritual and practical needs of the family, and offer suggestions on ways that the family can live a healthy and holy life.

Online Resources

Letters to the Family: Six customizable English and Spanish sample family letters are provided online. Sending letters home to parents is one way to keep them actively involved in their child's learning. There is a "Begin the Year" letter and one for each unit of every book.

Catholic Parenting 101: A wide variety of parent resources are also available online at RCLBFamilyLife.com offering articles and tips to help parents to fulfill their role as the primary educators of their children. These materials are updated frequently and cover a wide variety of topics such as parenting skills, spirituality in the home, keeping children safe, and speaking to children about difficult topics.

What Is a *Family Life* Catechist?

As a catechist or religion teacher you teach children about the Catholic faith and give witness to what you believe. You assist in the faith formation of the young people entrusted to your care. You join a long line of dedicated believers who have answered God's call to share their faith with others. Like these past catechists, you have been touched by your experience of Jesus Christ and are unable to keep the Good News to yourself.

In your role you assist parents in the faith formation of their children by making the teachings of the Catholic Church more explicit and helping the children to celebrate their faith and to apply the Church's teachings to their lives.

Catechists echo the Word of God to help others deepen their understanding of the faith. You may be a little daunted by this responsibility and ministry. You might even wonder if it is more than you bargained for when you were asked and accepted the invitation to teach this *Family Life* course. Relax! Great Saints and holy people, such as Moses, Jeremiah, Peter and Mary had similar concerns; but with God's help, they did great things—and you will too!

Qualities of a Catechist

The *National Directory for Catechesis* (NDC) published by the U.S. bishops in 2005 names key qualities of effective catechists and Catholic school religion teachers—qualities that you already possess. Catechists and religion teachers:

- ***Respond to a vocational call from the Lord*** to bring others to faith in him. As you catechize others you also continue to grow in your own faith and in your own knowledge of the faith.
- ***Give witness to the Gospel message of Jesus Christ*** as taught by his Church. You believe in this message and in her power to change the lives of all who believe in it. You model for others what it means to follow Jesus.
- ***Make a commitment to the Church*** to express the teachings of the Catholic Church as clearly and accurately as you can. You grow in understanding of the Catholic faith as you teach the Church's wisdom.
- ***Build a faith community among your learners*** because you have experienced its importance in your own life, through parish life and through your love of and participation in the Eucharist. You encourage and prepare your students

to live virtuous lives of forgiveness, reconciliation and peacemaking.

- ***Implement the mission of the Church*** to proclaim the Gospel to the world by responding to the needs of others and by teaching your students to do the same.
- ***Develop the skills and abilities needed*** to conduct effective catechetical sessions, present complex concepts so that they are clearly understood, and care for your students appropriately.

You can read more about the catechetical ministry in chapters 2 and 8 of the *National Directory for Catechesis*.

Qualities of a *Family Life* Catechist

In addition to the qualities of catechists and religion teachers named in the NDC, the *Family Life* catechist will also show in particular a:

- ***Dialogic Partnership with Families.*** The RCL Benziger *Family Life* series recognizes and celebrates the parents' primary role and responsibility in guiding their children's formation in all topics, not just those related to family life education. The *Family Life* catechist is to respect the parents' role and be willing to assist them in fulfilling this role in whatever ways they can. The *Family Life* catechist uses all means possible to keep parents informed about what the children are learning and to assist parents in helping their children integrate what they have learned into the family's life. Catechists will encourage parent participation and communication, and will listen attentively when parents speak. As much as possible, they will try to implement the parents' wishes for their children.
- ***Sensitivity to Diverse Family Settings.*** Children live in many diverse settings. Some live with their biological mothers and fathers; some are adopted. Some children live in families affected by divorce; others in families affected by sickness or death. Some have many siblings; others have none. The *Family Life* catechist will know their students well and will be sensitive to their home situations. When the program emphasizes the Church's teaching on the Christian family, the *Family Life* catechist will help the students to understand the blessings found in all families.
- ***Comfort with Human Sexuality.*** Although the program is designed so that parents may teach issues of human reproduction in the home, the RCL Benziger *Family Life* series, in every grade level, still presents the Church's teachings on human sexuality in age-appropriate ways. The *Family Life* catechist needs to be able to speak about these topics with dignity and grace. The catechist must believe that the human body is a sacred gift from God, and is something to be treated with respect and admiration, and not with fear or guilt. The catechist needs to be able to talk with their students without feeling awkwardness or shame, and must welcome the curious questions of children openly and responsibly. Teaching tips throughout the series will help you to do so in appropriate ways respecting prudence and modesty.

What Will I Teach?

Each grade level is organized around the same five themes. Each of these unit themes are presented according to the student's developmental readiness and level of comprehension. Each unit extends into the home through a variety of special parent materials.

Theme 1—God's Gift of Family

[T]he family has the mission to guard, reveal and communicate love, and this is a living reflection of and a real sharing in God's love for humanity and the love of Christ the Lord for the Church His bride.

FAMILIARIS CONSORTIO 17

Family living is the initial theme of the program, setting the context to explore all the themes. In every grade, students will develop the skills and knowledge they need to live a healthy and holy life within their family, for now and in the future. Students will develop these key Catholic values in association with this theme:

- An appreciation that the family is the person's first community
- An understanding that beliefs and values are developed, shared and lived within the family
- An awareness that healthy families provide social and spiritual meaning for all members
- A recognition that each family member is responsible for the life of the Catholic family

Theme 2—God's Gift of Self

Ideally, each person strives to be physically developed, psychologically integrated, interpersonally responsible, and spiritually holy. [In addition, there is] the wider, more universal calling to be loving and chaste, whatever one's vocation is in life.

HUMAN SEXUALITY PAGE 26

In this unit, students will be challenged to understand the physical, emotional and spiritual development of themselves and others. They will also learn to examine their motives honestly, and appreciate their strengths and weaknesses. Through these efforts, they will grow in realistic self-esteem, a valuable component of a person's emotional health and a valuable tool to overcome negative peer pressure and temptations within the culture. Students will develop these key Catholic values in association with this theme:

- An understanding of how to express their emotions appropriately
- A responsible attitude toward one's physical health and care of the body
- A sense of self as a gift necessary to form healthy relationships
- An awareness that spiritual growth is a life-long process, just like physical and emotional development
- The formation of their conscience, shaped by authentic Church teaching, that will help them to make good moral choices

Theme 3—God's Gift of Life

At this tense moment in our history, when external wars and internal violence make us so conscious of death, an affirmation of the sanctity of human life by renewed attention to the family is imperative. HUMAN LIFE IN OUR DAY 83

In this unit, students will grow in their appreciation of the sacredness of human life and of their own potential to love and serve selflessly.

Students will develop these key Catholic values in association with this theme:

- A reverence for human life, and all that supports and contributes to it
- An understanding of the inherent dignity of the human person as created in God's image and likeness, regardless of productivity, role, function, or social status
- A recognition that every stage of human life, from conception until natural death, is precious
- An awareness of the challenges that exist to the sanctity of life and the moral strength required from every person in order to respond to these challenges

Theme 4—God's Gift of Love

> *Like all our human powers and freedoms, sexuality, a gift from God, can be channeled for good or ill. Each of us is entrusted by God with the responsibility to guide and direct this gift wisely and lovingly.* HUMAN SEXUALITY PAGE 10

In this unit, students will develop gradually a wholesome understanding of sexuality and its place in Catholic family life. They will learn, as appropriate by their age, that human sexuality is intimately connected with the gifts of love and life, with strength and service, with compassion and discipline. Through lessons on healthy habits and moral virtues, they will learn the need to live healthy and holy lives. Students will develop these key Catholic values in association with this theme:

- An appreciation of the critical role gender has in the life of every person
- An understanding of the importance of the virtue of chastity and healthy attitudes about sexuality for living a moral life
- A respect for the reproductive abilities of the human body and its connection to full personhood and family life

Theme 5—God's Gift of Community

> *The truth of globalization as a process and its fundamental ethical criterion are given by the unity of the human family and its development towards what is good. Hence a sustained commitment is needed so as to* promote a person-based and community-oriented cultural process of world-wide integration that is open to transcendence.
>
> CARITAS IN VERITATE 42

The family, as the domestic Church, is one of the key communities in which people live as disciples of Jesus and where discipleship is taught. An understanding of how people live with and relate to one another is an essential component of discipleship and family living. In this unit, students will learn the virtues and skills needed for a just society. These lessons will prepare them to take their responsible places in society both now and in the future. Students will learn how to answer the call to Christian social ministry. Students will develop these key Catholic values in association with this theme:

- A respect for interpersonal relationships and human interaction
- An appreciation for the cooperation and mutual benefit needed for a healthy society
- A willingness to implement Catholic Social Teaching such as solidarity and stewardship
- A recognition for all Christians to work together for the coming of God's reign of justice, mercy and peace

How Will I Teach?

> *Under the guidance of the Holy Spirit, catechists powerfully influence those being catechized by their faithful proclamation of the Gospel of Jesus Christ and the transparent example of their Christian lives.*
>
> National Directory For Catechesis 29E

The catechetical ministry has been nurtured and renewed in recent years by the publication of three documents: The *Catechism of the Catholic Church* (1993), the *General Directory for Catechesis* (1997), and the *National Directory for Catechesis* (2005).

The *Catechism of the Catholic Church* (CCC) provides a systematic presentation of the contents of the Catholic faith. The *General Directory for Catechesis* (GDC) defines the goals, principles and guidelines of catechesis. The *National Directory for Catechesis* (NDC) applies these principles of catechesis to catechetical ministry in the United States. The RCL Benziger *Family Life* series reflects these key documents throughout.

Divine Methodology

The *National Directory for Catechesis*, in chapter 4, examines the use of methodology in catechesis. Beginning with the divine methodology (God's self-Revelation to us through Jesus and the Holy Spirit), the NDC reminds us that God has revealed everything we know and believe about our faith. Catechists are encouraged to follow this methodology by engaging "persons and communities in light of their circumstances and their capacity to accept and interpret Revelation" (NDC 28).

Human Methodologies

The second part of chapter 4 of the National Directory focuses on the elements of human methodology. It emphasizes that, because learning takes place in different ways, we should rely on a variety of methods to pass on our faith to students, just as God has done. The NDC offers eight different human methodologies that catechists can use (see NDC 29 A-H). All eight are featured throughout the RCL Benziger *Family Life* series.

1. ***Learning through Human Experience:*** We respond to God's invitation through our human experiences. Each RCL Benziger *Family Life* lesson begins by engaging the child's interest and imagination and helping them relate the lesson concept to their own experiences.

2. ***Learning by Discipleship:*** We learn the Way of Jesus Christ by choosing to follow him and do what he asks us. In each lesson students are introduced to Jesus' teaching and learn how to live and act as Jesus' disciples.

3. ***Learning within the Christian Community:*** The witness of the Church shows children how to believe, worship and take up the Gospel call to service. In each lesson, students are taught the skills that will help them to live as responsible members of the Catholic Church.

4. ***Learning within the Christian Family:*** The Christian family is usually the first experience children have of living within community. The family offers the first and best environment for growth in faith. RCL Benziger *Family Life* fosters a partnership between home, school and parish. Students learn family living skills, and resources are provided to help families grow in faith, hope, and love together.

5. ***Learning through the Witness of the Catechist:*** You have a powerful influence on your students' faith formation. You influence them by the knowledge you share, by your attitudes and actions, and by the witness you give that your faith is important to you. You model for them what is important and what is not. You show them what it means to live a Christian life. RCL Benziger *Family Life* provides you with sure guidance on being a positive witness.

6. ***Learning by Heart:*** When we "learn by heart," we make knowledge or a skill our own. We have it in memory for life. Students develop a strong Catholic identity and literacy by learning key definitions, moral teachings, and Catholic practices and prayers. The Catholics Believe and Catholic Family Album features in RCL Benziger *Family Life* provide the students treasures of the Church that strengthen their Catholic identity.

7. ***Making a Commitment to Live the Christian Life:*** Faith statements remain merely words until students make a commitment to live them out in their own lives. In every lesson the RCL Benziger *Family Life* series invites students to make a concrete choice and commitment to act upon what they have learned.

8. ***Learning by Apprenticeship:*** Children are quick studies: they watch what adults and older children do, and then they imitate what they have seen. This imitation is at the heart of learning by apprenticeship. Students are encouraged to find adults whom they can trust and learn from. Learning approaches used within each lesson encourage students to learn from others and to practice imitating moral, healthy and holy behavior.

Know Your Eighth Graders

Whether you are a seasoned professional teacher or a first-year catechist, it's always good to stop now and then, place yourself in the shoes of your students, and imagine who they are. What are their abilities? How do they view themselves, you, their families, and the world? The thumbnail sketch on this page offers some general characteristics of thirteen-year-olds drawn from current research. Only you and the child's parents, after careful observation and dialogue with your students, can know the extent to which each of your students corresponds to this norm. So get to know your students well.

Physical and Emotional Characteristics

- There are many changes taking place during this stage of development, many of them individually. Be aware of the variety and who is and isn't affected. This can be a source of tension within this age group.
- Eighth graders value peer acceptance and find it important to belong.
- They are going through a time of profound moral development and questioning. Eighth graders need opportunities to talk through and think about issues.
- They want to be trusted and to take on greater responsibilities.
- They are protective of their privacy.

Learning Skills

- They can focus attention and time to search for needed information.
- They can develop a plan and meet a goal.
- They enjoy cooperative learning strategies where they work with others on a task or project.
- They generally have well-developed verbal skills.
- Their increased attention span allows for more concentrated development of concepts.

Religious Growth

- They have a well-defined sense of justice.
- They enjoy participating in discussions, celebrations, and prayer services held in an atmosphere of safety and love.
- Eighth graders may wonder what meaning the Church has in their lives.
- Faith development happens best within groups and communities where they feel like they belong.

Conclusion

All of these qualities and abilities affect the child's role in the family as well. They are no longer children and yet, do not have the responsibilities and privileges of adults. This may cause strain on the parent-child relationship as eighth graders yearn for more freedom from parents who are not yet ready to loosen the reins. They know the rules and know when they have fallen short of the mark. They can better understand their parent's point of view, although they frequently question it. They can take more responsibility for younger siblings, and begin to serve as role models for them. As they begin to take the responsibility that comes with freedom, you can help them develop good decision-making skills by helping them to critically reflect on moral decisions they will be facing. These critical reflection skills can help students become more responsible members of their families and society.

Partnering with the Family

The classroom has become the setting for most curricula, and too many family materials are designed to support the classroom teaching. Gradually the family's central role of overseeing the moral development of their children has been eroded. RCL Benziger *Family Life* changes that equation and puts the parents back in their primary and essential role. The *Family Life* materials help to foster a partnership between the family and the parish that is needed for successful faith formation.

The Home

Parents are the first and most influential shapers of their children's moral values and character. The Catholic Church has consistently called for parents to reclaim this role and has offered them assistance in doing so. "The Church holds that it is her duty to give parents back confidence in their own capabilities and help them to carry out their task" (*The Truth and Meaning of Human Sexuality* 47). RCL Benziger *Family Life* places the home and the parents at the center of the program. Parents can use the RCL Benziger *Family Life* materials with confidence knowing that they conform to and implement appropriate Church documents, and that they have been found to be in conformity with the *Catechism of the Catholic Church*.

The School and Parish

Several Church documents call for parishes and schools to support parents in their role as moral educators. RCL Benziger *Family Life* provides the essential resources needed to provide a substantial and effective moral catechesis for all children.

The Child

The child is at the heart of all family life education. RCL Benziger *Family Life* introduces children to the Catholic Church's moral teachings as they apply to family living, helps them to understand these teachings appropriately by age, and teaches practical ways to follow these teachings in making moral decisions.

The *Family Life* program assures children of their worth and dignity, and helps them take pride in their families, regardless of its problems. Children are affirmed in their human dignity at each stage of development. They are taught to make good moral decisions by applying sound moral principles and skills. They are challenged to deepen their moral perspective and to take on greater responsibility each year. Most importantly, children develop the habits (living the virtues) and build the skills they need to live healthy and holy moral lives. RCL Benziger *Family Life* provides young people with the foundation they will need in the future as they respond to God's call to love their way through life.

Child Safety Education

This edition of the RCL Benziger *Family Life* has been revised to assist parishes and dioceses in their effort to implement the 2002 *Charter for the Protection of Children*. The *Family Life* series supports safe environment training to the Church's children and youth, and to provide support to parents and teachers who are responsible for the education and safety of the children. This revision puts into practice this advice from the National Center for Missing and Exploited Children (NCMEC):

> Programs on child safety . . . should be designed to increase children's ability to recognize and avoid potentially dangerous situations and help better protect themselves. Equally important is the development of self-esteem at every level of the educational process, because children with self-confidence are less likely to be victimized. (*Guidelines for Programs to Reduce Child Victimization* page 4.)

RCL Benziger *Family Life* integrates child safety education into a holistic approach to family life education. In every lesson of every grade level, children are provided with opportunities to develop the knowledge, self-confidence, and assertiveness skills that they will need to recognize dangerous situations, avoid them if possible, and respond appropriately in time of need.

RCL Benziger *Family Life* is also designed to help reduce guilt feelings among children, encourage them to speak frequently and freely with their parents and other trusted adults, express their feelings appropriately, and to practice forgiving themselves and others. All of these items reflect the best of safe environment educational theory.

The Importance of Repetition and Reinforcement

According to research commissioned by the NCMEC, the most successful child safety programs were those that were offered over a significant period of time and provided children multiple opportunities to learn, interact with and apply the rules of child safety. These programs taught children how to recognize, avoid and protect themselves from dangerous situations, modeled for the children appropriate behavior, had the children actively rehearse that behavior, and provided consistent feedback and reinforcement.

Children are given multiple opportunities over the ten lessons within each grade level to learn, interact with and apply the rules of child safety in an interactive manner as recommended by NCMEC. RCL Benziger *Family Life* meets the criteria and addresses the skills identified as important by the NCMEC. According to NCMEC, such education should teach children:

- Basic safety rules in an age appropriate manner.
- The difference between appropriate and inappropriate touching.
- To say "No" to any touch or action that causes them to feel unwelcome, uncomfortable, or confused.

- How to respond to situations that cause them fear or discomfort.
- The importance of open and honest communication with parents or guardians, and of identifying people they can trust in times when they need to talk to someone besides their parents

The child safety component of RCL Benziger *Family Life* has been carefully integrated into the series so that child safety issues and skills are seen as a normal part of the family life curriculum. Because parents have the primary responsibility for their children's safety, this series is designed to work in partnership with them.

Materials are designed so that parents can teach these important topics in the home or practice them once they have been taught in the school or religious education program. While the responsibility for protecting children from harm falls primarily on adults, children have the right to safety training and parishes have the obligation to provide such training. Protecting children helps to define us as a Church: Catholics protect children, provide them with a safe environment, and teach children what they can do to protect themselves.

You, as teacher or catechist, also have an essential role in supporting the parents. While you may not feel adequately prepared for your role, do not let that discourage you from moving ahead. Remember, you are teaching children the skills they need to protect themselves from harm.

Child Safety

Here are some basic rules to remember when teaching children safety issues:

- Avoid frightening the child.
- Use stories and examples to communicate the message, rather than lecturing.
- Show children how to respond to various situations and then practice what you show them.
- Listen carefully to what children say; teach them that adults will listen to and believe them.
- Help children feel good about themselves.
- Help them to understand that they are not responsible for the actions of adults or others.
- Avoid anything that might make children feel guilty because of the actions of others.

Catechetical Formation in Chaste Living

In November 2007 the United States Conference of Catholic Bishops approved the document *Catechetical Formation in Chaste Living: Guidelines for Curriculum Design and Publication*. Accordingly, the RCL Benziger *Family Life* series has been developed in conformity with the requirements of this document.

Created by the USCCB Committee on Catechesis (now the Committee on Evangelization and Catechesis), the Chaste Living guidelines were built upon the foundation laid by recent Church documents, namely, *Catechism of the Catholic Church, General Directory for Catechesis, National Directory for Catechesis,* and *United States Catholic Catechism for Adults*. These Chaste Living guidelines were also formed through a series of national consultations on the document. Through this consultation process, all the bishops of the United States and members of their catechetical and pastoral ministry staffs offered corrections and changes to the document. Theologians, catechists, and experts in chaste living education also participated in this process by which the final document was produced.

The introduction to the guidelines ends with these words:

> [T]he Church continues to proclaim salvation in Christ Jesus and to invite men and women to follow his way. Though humanity is still wounded by sin, the Church continues to call all to trust in God's mercy, to turn away from sin, and to embrace the Good News. She continues to teach everyone how to live as Jesus did, instructing them in the message of the Ten Commandments, the Beatitudes, and the entire Gospel. She urges frequent reception of the sacraments, especially Penance and Reconciliation and the Eucharist, and cultivation of the virtues that enable people to lead a chaste and holy life (pg. 2).

The Chaste Living guidelines state that education for chaste living is essential to the formation of children and adolescents in the Catholic faith and "should be mandatory in Catholic schools and in parish religious education and youth ministry programs. This may be done in the form of a curriculum, a presentation for youth and/or parents, or the use of other educational materials" (pg. 1).

This too is the vision and purpose of the RCL Benziger *Family Life* series: (1) to proclaim the salvation of Jesus and invite people to a life as his disciples; (2) to call people to trust in God's mercy, turn away from sin, and embrace the Good News; (3) to instruct people in the Church's moral teachings; (4) to encourage active participation in the Church's sacramental and worship life; and (5) to help people to cultivate the virtues so that they may live chaste and holy lives.

To help parishes, school, and programs of youth ministry accomplish this mandate, this series provides a variety of options for presenting the material, including classroom sessions, teaching at home, and large group intergenerational gatherings.

Here are some of the ways the RCL Benziger *Family Life* series implements the directives in the U.S. Bishops' document:

- The series was developed following the *Catechism of the Catholic Church*, the *General Directory for Catechesis*, and the *National Directory for Catechesis*.
- Catechesis on Catholic faith and morals and on the virtues is presented as an essential part of every lesson.
- All catechesis on chaste living takes place within the faith community.
- Catechists and teachers are seen as assisting parents in the formation of their children.
- Catechists and teachers are provided with a clear knowledge of Catholic teaching.
- Parents are provided with the resources they need to fulfill their particular responsibility to catechize their children in faith and morals. Tips are provided throughout the take-home and online resources and the Parent Connection booklets to help prepare parents to speak to the issues addressed throughout the series.
- Parents are recognized as having the primary role of providing specific education in human sexuality. Human Reproduction Booklet A and Human Reproduction Booklet B are provided for two levels so that parents can explain human sexuality at home. These booklets are generally used during the fifth and sixth grade, when the children are entering puberty; but these two booklets can be used at older grades levels as well. Proper references are made to human anatomy or physiology, but only to the degree necessary to teach morality and virtuous living.

Learning Outcomes for Chaste Living

In writing this document, the U.S. Bishops desired that each baptized person:

- cherish human dignity as made in the image and likeness of God.
- faithfully reflect that image in a life conformed to new life in Christ.
- deepen the relationship with Christ and the Church through frequent prayer and celebration of the Sacraments, especially the Sacrament of Penance and Reconciliation and the Sacrament of the Eucharist.
- embrace joyfully the call to love and live chastely either as a married person or as a celibate person.

Each of these desired outcomes is promoted within every level of the RCL Benziger *Family Life* series.

Models for Implementation of RCL Benziger *Family Life*

In Catholic Schools

Most Catholic schools offer the *Family Life* series in ten teaching blocks, corresponding with the ten lessons in each grade level. Any one of the following three models can help you implement the program into your existing curriculum. Detailed instructions for using each of these is provided in the Program Director's Manual.

Two-Week Course

Set aside two weeks during the year and teach one lesson per day during the regularly scheduled religion class. The lesson plans provided in the Teacher Edition are designed to be taught in a 45-minute class period. There are also plenty of suggestions for how to expand the lesson for longer class sessions. This approach provides a special emphasis on family life curriculum and enables you to actively engage parents during this time.

Ten-Week Course

Teach this series during your regular religion class one day a week over a period of ten weeks. Pick a day during the week so that students will become accustomed to having the lessons on the same day. For example, if you pick Thursday, the students will know they will have a *Family Life* lesson on Thursdays. Parents will also come to expect this consistency and will learn to set aside time before, during and after the lesson is taught in order to reinforce what has been learned.

Ten-Month Course

This approach allows you to reinforce family life curriculum throughout the entire school year. Designate one day a month as Family Life Day. A lesson from the *Family Life* series would be taught during the scheduled religion class, and all other classes would emphasize the importance of engaging the family. On this day, celebrate the family in a variety of ways. Use the *Family Life* series as an opportunity to engage families more actively in the life of your school and in the life of their children.

In the Parish

Finding time within the catechetical year calendar can be challenging. However, because of the its flexibility, the *Family Life* series can be used without taking away from the time needed for regular religious instruction. Detailed instructions for using each of these models is provided in the Program Director's Manual.

Supplement to Religion Period

Add thirty minutes to a regular religion period ten times a year. This approach will enable you to flow from the regular lesson into the *Family Life* lesson. A correlation chart is available online at RCLBFamilyLife.com showing how *Family Life* can be integrated into your religion curriculum.

Condense into Five Sessions

Each grade level of *Family Life* is organized into five units. This makes it possible to condense the teaching of the ten lessons into five sessions. Lesson plans are provided in the Program Director's Manual detailing how this can best be accomplished.

Summer Program

Promote and strengthen family life during your summer programming. Include one hour each day for *Family Life*. Encourage family members to actively participate in their children's studies.

Intergenerational Sessions

Bring families together for five evenings during the year for a Family Life Night. Schedule a two-hour session for family activities and lessons taken from *Family Life*. Lesson plans are provided in the Program Director's Manual for teaching a unit in one lesson.

Scope and Sequence for Grade 

	God's Gift of Family	God's Gift of Self	God's Gift of Life	God's Gift of Love	God's Gift of Community
Faith Concepts	God has placed in the human heart the natural desire for happiness; With an informed conscience and free will, we can choose to follow the right path to happiness	Each person is an unique individual created with a soul, an intellect and free will; The Theological Virtue of hope opens up a person's heart to desire and expect the happiness	Each person has a fundamental dignity because everyone has been created in the image and likeness of God; Sin and moral evil are at the root of the many threats against human life	Human sexuality is primarily concerned with our capacity to love and form relationships based on being male or female; Married love is to be self-giving and life-giving	God created us as social beings; therefore, we need to experience a healthy sense of belonging; Life has meaning with a God-given purpose
Virtues	Gratitude; Counsel	Confidence; Valor	Respect; Good judgment	Modesty; Fidelity	Vigilance; Responsibility
Family Skills	Developing communica-tion skills; Making an examination of conscience	Keeping a journal; Managing emotions	Assessing personal attitudes; Practicing good healthy choices	Practicing skills for building respectful friendships; Witnessing Fruits of the Holy Spirit	Practicing social skills; Planning for the future
Catholic Family Album	Saint Jude Thaddeus; Saint Anne	Saint Albert Chmielowski: Saint Joan of Arc	Cyber Bridges; Saint Maximilian Kolbe	Saint John of the Cross; Blessed Zélie Martin	Saint John Bosco; Saint Hildegard von Bingen
Catechism of the Catholic Church	CCC 1718–1724, 1776–1794	CCC 356–368, 1817–1821	CCC 1700–1709, 2258, 2284–2291	CCC 1601, 1641, 2332	CCC 68, 1877–1880, 1939–1942

UNIT 1

God's Gift of Family

Background

*"The family, which is founded and given life by love, is a community of persons: of husband and wife, of parents and children, of relatives. Its first task is to live with fidelity the reality of communion in a constant effort to develop an authentic community of persons. The inner principle of that task, its permanent power and its final goal is love" (*Familiaris Consortio *18).*

GOD CREATED LIFE IN US BECAUSE WE ARE LOVED by him. The primary arena where God's love is first experienced is in the family. We painfully know that this does not always happen. Humans are weak and capable of sin. We can make decisions that are harmful to ourselves and others.

Nevertheless, the goal of family life in God's plan remains unchanged: we are called to live in love. Our response to this call is the source of genuine happiness. Sharing the gift of love with each other in the many settings of family life is a sure way to fulfill God's plan for us.

God wishes to share his life and love with us— forever. That is why God freely chose to create us, to share the gift of divine love with us. God desires us to be happy, yet we cannot create happiness ourselves. Adam and Eve gave that a try, and we all know the result. Happiness is not something we can create outside of our relationship with God. True happiness is the choice of living in accord with the dignity and the direction that God has set for us.

Additional Background

Catechism of the Catholic Church: §§ 1657, 1882, 2201–2203, 2205, 2225–2226, 2685

GIFTS FROM GOD ARE GIVEN TO BE SHARED. Sharing with others what we have received from God is one of the most sanctified ways of responding in gratitude to God for all his gifts and blessings. When we turn inward and hoard our blessings and gifts, we deprive ourselves of experiencing the blessings that are connected with the gift of love. When we neglect our responsibilities to others, we fail to follow the way of love, the way that God intends for all of us. We lose direction in life and become lost.

The gift of freedom is among the greatest gifts that have been given to us by God. All of us, especially those who are young, need direction to use the gift of freedom well. Young people need the guidance of wise parents and teachers.

The family is the school of virtue, the school where we learn the good habit of using our gift of freedom and our other gifts wisely for our own well-being and the well-being of others. In the family our conscience is formed and trained. Solid Christian education or catechesis can also serve this need. These tasks are a challenge for the family, especially when many young people are looking elsewhere for guidance.

FAMILY FORMATION LASTS A LIFETIME.
Affirming the importance of family life is an affirmation of the basics. The value of family is the starting point for family life education. Yet, there are those who downgrade the significance of the family or consider it an obsolete social institution. As one begins to teach young adolescents about the importance of family relationships, know that your enthusiasm for family life will be your most important asset in this educational venture.

For Reflection

Read and reflect on the following:
"[T]he family, in which the various generations come together and help one another to grow wiser . . . is the foundation of society" (Gaudium et Spes *52).*

- What are some of the things that my family does to create a place where we live as a community supporting one another?
- What can I do to help my students experience our "class" as a community of learning and sharing?

Child Safety

The three key words in child safety education are these: Recognize, Respond and Report. Your task is to help the students recognize those situations and behaviors that have the potential to cause them harm. Next, the students need to understand what steps they can take to avoid or to deal with these possibly dangerous situations. Finally, students need to understand the importance of telling their parents or another trusted adult about the dangerous situation and how they dealt with it.

Family Time

Family Focus

Families with children at this age often feel the tension between maintaining a vital family life and the pull from the outside. This can be a healthy creative tension. Still, treasure all family moments whether they be around the dinner table, in front of the television, on the way to a ball game or whenever you are together. Live fully in those moments by appreciating each member of the family. Encourage the parents of your students to use the Family Time pages to help appreciate those moments together.

UNIT 1
God's Gift of Family
Family Time
Walking in God's Way
Family Blessings
Healthy Habits In the Home
Making Connections
Faith on the Fridge

LESSON 1 PLANNER

Goal: To examine ways to contribute to family happiness and develop the skills to show respect, affirmation and generosity as means of expressing gratitude

Engage
Page 33

Objective
To explore the meaning of happiness

Family Time
Ensure that each student tears out their Family Time page to complete at home.

Pray
Psalm 34:5–11

Focus
Survey experiences of homemade moments.

Discover
Discuss the source of happiness.

Teach
Page 34

Objective
To understand basic human needs and how to express gratitude

Focus
Rank essential needs in life.

Explore
Read, discuss and summarize the importance of meeting needs as part of contributing to personal happiness.
Growing in Virtue: Gratitude

Connect
Catholics Believe: Happiness is a natural desire.
Communicate gratitude for a favorite moment of the week.

Apply
Page 36

Objective
To practice skills that can contribute to family happiness

Focus
Continuum line on responsibility

Discover
Catholic Family Album: Saint Jude Thaddeus

Integrate
Evaluate situations to see how to make family life happier.

Pray
Prayer for the intercession of Saint Jude

Vocabulary Preview

Affirmation—the skill of acknowledging the importance of someone through honest praise, which encourages them to do their best

Generosity—the capacity to be giving or sharing of what we have and who we are; entails humility and sacrifice

Gratitude—the capacity and ability to choose to be appreciative of all that one receives

Respect—a sign and attitude that values another's personhood, needs, feelings and gifts as important

Materials Needed

- writing paper
- pens, pencils
- art supplies
- Bible
- Lesson 1 Activity Masters

Call to Prayer

Lord, you fashioned families to help us live in a healthy, happy, holy way. Help me to teach my students ways to reach for happiness by generous giving to others. Help them to learn the skills to build healthy relationships. Amen.

Homegrown Happiness

Something in Common

"Best summer vacation," Peter challenged his friends.

"Hawaii, last year!" Rachel shouted, waving a French fry. The others chimed in with their own personal "bests."

Sitting around a table at the mall, sharing burgers and fries, the group of friends had already listed their favorite songs, movies, and games.

Then Erica, who had been quietly sipping her lemonade, spoke up. "Best moment this week," she said.

The giggles tapered off. This was worth thinking about.

Pete took up the challenge first. "That's pretty easy for me," he answered. "It's got to be finally having my own computer." Everyone knew times had been tough in Pete's home lately, but were finally getting better.

"My best moment isn't that huge," Erica said. "But I did get through my dance recital on Tuesday without falling on my face. My mom looked so proud of me!"

Josh looked up from the table, where he had been texting on his phone. "I've been texting my Uncle Phil about when we might visit him in Arizona. I miss him, but we stay connected. He enjoys playing games online, like I do. So cool!"

"My turn," Rachel said. "And I can tell you exactly when it happened. It was Monday afternoon, and we were all in the waiting room at the hospital. The doctor came in and told us my brother didn't have cancer after all! I just yelled, 'Thank you, God!'"

This lesson will help you to:
- **explore** the meaning of happiness.
- **understand** basic human needs and how to express gratitude.
- **practice** skills that can contribute to family happiness.

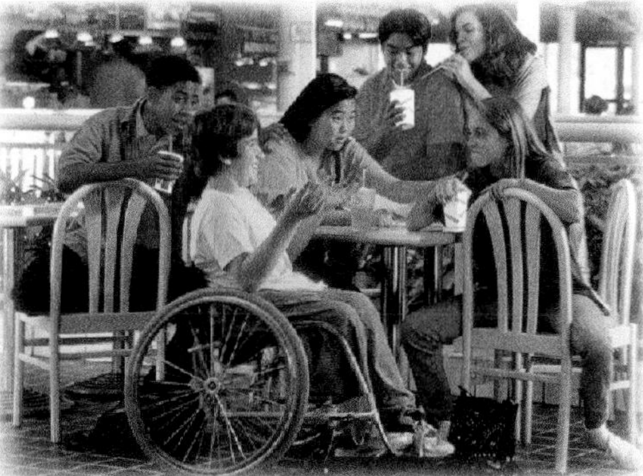

What was your happiest moment this week?

Homegrown Happiness 11

Teaching Tip

Child Safety: You will find child safety teaching suggestions embedded within each of the lessons of this course. Safe environment training gives children the helpful skills to play their part in protecting themselves from would-be offenders. The key skills, put into play in various ways appropriate to the children's ages, are those that help the child RECOGNIZE inappropriate behavior, RESPOND to it effectively, and REPORT the situation to a trusted adult. Teach the children to recognize when they feel unsafe or uncomfortable using examples from their lives. Practice saying "no." Help them list who are trusted adults in their lives.

Objective

To explore the meaning of happiness

Pray

Open the lesson by prayerfully reading Psalm 34:5–11.

Focus

Ask volunteers to give examples for: homemade, homegrown and home cooking. Survey the class to see which kind of meal they prefer: a fast food meal or a home-cooked meal? Have them share reasons for their choices.

Discover

- Read "Something in Common." Allow students to ask questions and share insights about the reading.
- Have students role-play the story. During the dialogue, have students write on the board what they think the source of happiness is for each character in the story.
- Pair up students to share their happiest moment this week. Have them identify its source. Then have the class discuss the common sources for their happiness.
- Explain that happiness is found more in relationships rather than in material things.
- Time permitting, have students in small groups define happiness by completing the statement: Happiness is . . .

TEACH

Objective

To understand basic human needs and how to express gratitude

Focus

- Gather students in groups to develop and rank ten essential needs in life. Then consolidate the groups' lists into one class list of the top five needs.
- Compare the top five needs with popular ads. See if students can identify an ad that addresses each of the five top needs.

Explore

- Have students quietly read "Family Matters." As the class then reads the text aloud, pause for students to react or ask questions.
- Direct students to see how their top five needs relate to physical, emotional, intellectual and spiritual needs. Have them fill in any missing gaps in their top needs lists.
- Privately have each student assess whether their top needs are met, neglected or over-gratified. Inquire: How do you respond when your needs and wants are met?
- Discuss with students what makes people happy. Help them to recognize that they are not responsible for the happiness of others. They should be concerned when others depend upon them in order to be happy. Encourage students to speak with a trusted adult adviser in such situations.

Note: The multi-colored dotted box contains child safety content.

Catholics Believe

God has placed in the human heart the natural desire for happiness. The Beatitudes respond to this desire in order to draw us closer to God, who is the ultimate fulfillment of all happiness.

Family Matters

The group of friends in the story felt happy about some of the things that were going on in their lives. They felt that certain needs they had were being met. There is a reason why they believed that their family members were part of their happiness. For most people the first place their important needs are met is in their family. Families help us meet our physical, emotional, intellectual, and spiritual needs.

As a human being you share certain basic needs with everyone else. You have physical needs for food, shelter, security, and care. You also have emotional needs that include, for example, the need to feel supported.

Yet you are not just a body with feelings. You also have intellectual needs to explore, create, and understand. And finally, you have spiritual needs because you are a whole person, body and soul. When your spiritual needs are met through prayer, reflection, worship, participation in the celebration of the Eucharist and other Sacraments, and service to others, you can discover happiness in life.

Some of the things families do together can make happiness easier to achieve. Happiness does not just happen to us. happiness is a choice. Like the group of friends in the story, we need to take time to reflect on the events of our lives to see what we have experienced that contributes to our happiness.

We also need to have gratitude. In other words, when we reflect on life, we need to discover and see the good in life and not be overcome by the "not so happy events." Showing gratitude is a skill that we can practice and improve upon.

Think about those things in life for which you are grateful.

Gathering to discuss favorite moments with family and friends in life is a wonderful way to practice expressing our gratitude. When we choose to appreciate what we have received, we realize life is good. This is at the heart of happiness.

12 Homegrown Happiness

Teaching Tip

Child Safety: Young teens, in particular, have a great need to be liked and accepted. Their happiness is aided by the kind words they receive from others. Sexual abusers will often take advantage of a young person's desire to please, using it to "groom" them for sexual activity. Help students understand that while their behaviors, attitudes and actions can affect others' feelings, they are neither responsible for another's happiness or sadness, nor are they capable of making another happy or sad. Help them to see that expecting another to make them happy and taking responsibility for another's happiness are emotionally unhealthy behaviors. Help them to identify healthy and unhealthy behaviors.

We cannot and do not always feel happy. When you feel worried or sad, upset or angry, turn to God. Share your feelings with him. He is the source of our happiness.

Everyone wants to be around a happy person. In part, this is why we love sharing best moments, favorite things, or telling funny or memorable moments in our life. Life is more enjoyable when there is happiness because happiness is contagious.

To improve your ability to be grateful, focus and practice on these key qualities of happiness:

- **Respect.** Respect is a sign and attitude that we consider one another's needs, feelings, and gifts as important.
- **Affirmation.** Affirmation is the skill of acknowledging the importance of someone. Honest praise and healthy pride encourage others to do their best.
- **Generosity.** Generosity is the capacity to be giving or sharing of what we have and who we are. This entails humility and sacrifice.

Growing in Virtue

Gratitude is both an attitude and a skill. It is a good habit, or virtue, that we need to practice and communicate. The more we show gratitude in life and for life, we discover the happier we really are—and will be.

"Communicating Gratitude"

Write about your favorite moment this week. Then share your gratitude for that experience with a partner and at home. Be sure to include the key qualities of happiness.

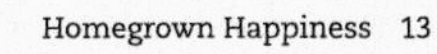

Extending the Lesson

Using Activity Master 1A: Use the Activity Master "Needs and Happiness." This activity will help students analyze a given situation to determine what need is met. There is also an opportunity to provide a personal example.

Guest Speaker: Invite a parish staff member or volunteer to talk with the students about ways the parish helps families meet their needs. Ask the speaker to focus on all major aspects of our needs (physical, emotional, intellectual and spiritual). Ask the speaker to relate the parish ministries to the Corporal and Spiritual Works of Mercy. Encourage the speaker to also invite students to help in ways they can actively and effectively participate in these ministries as well as practice the skills of communicating with respect, affirmation and generosity.

- Encourage the youth to speak with a trusted adult advisor if they are ever pressured to do something uncomfortable or inappropriate to make another person happy.

- Read the Growing in Virtue box. Discuss why when a need of ours is met, we should be grateful.
- Inquire: How do you show or communicate gratitude or your happiness in life?

Connect

- Have students brainstorm words, gestures and actions that show a person has gratitude or is happy.
- Discuss how having a need met can result in gratitude. If a need is met, then I am to be thankful and can express it. The more we show gratitude, the happier we will be.
- Read the Catholics Believe box on the previous page. Explain that the desire for happiness is universal. Therefore, the key qualities of happiness apply to all in communicating gratitude.
- Have students complete the activity on the page. If needed, have them finish the activity at home with their family.
- Time permitting, invite students to discuss the impact of instant versus delayed gratification on a person's ability to show gratitude.

APPLY

To practice skills that can contribute to family happiness

Focus

Draw on the board a long horizontal line. On the left side write "little" and then on the right side "lots." Have students mark how responsible they are in given situations, such as, cleaning around the house, doing homework, etc. Then discuss the results.

Discover

Read the Catholic Family Album box. Ask: How does Saint Jude inspire gratitude? *(By spreading the Gospel with joy, he effectively contributed to others' happiness. By responding to prayers of people in need, he gives them hope and assurance of God's love.)*

Integrate

- Read "Doing My Share." Reinforce with students that they are still maturing and in many ways dependent upon their family.
- Have students complete the activity on the page. Share as a class the various responses.
- Time permitting, have them share how it might feel after they carry out some of their suggestions.

Pray

Pray a prayer to Saint Jude for his intercession.

Catholic Family Album

Saint Jude Thaddeus was one of the original Twelve Apostles. He was brother of James the Less and likely a relative of Jesus. People who are facing serious situations in their life often turn to Saint Jude in prayer. They pray for the strength of faith and hope to deal with their suffering. As the result of a vision, Saint Bridget of Sweden helped revive devotion to Saint Jude. She described him as "generous." Today St. Jude's Children Hospital in Memphis, Tennessee is known for amazing research and the treatment of diseases. They give hope to children afflicted by these diseases and their families.

Doing My Share

Happiness has little to do with the way we look or the things we have. Happiness is found in the love of God. God made us to love. And we often feel our best when we do the work of love. Jesus is our model for meeting other people's needs through love. When we reach out to others to help them meet their needs, we show them love.

Now that you are becoming more independent and growing in your responsibilities you can, more than ever before, help people in need around you—like your family and friends. You are old enough to begin to support the needs of others and practice the skill of showing your gratitude.

You can contribute to your own happiness as well as your family's happiness by how you choose to live your life. For each situation below, tell what you would do to help make family life happier.

1. Your mom is working a full-time job and also trying to keep up with all the needs around the house. She sometimes feels unappreciated and tired. **I would** ______________________________

2. You were the star player on your Little League team but your younger brother just cannot play well at all. Everyone expects him to be another you and they tease him about it. Nobody else seems to notice that he is really good at running track. **I would** ______________________________

3. Now choose a real situation and tell what you will do. When my family ______________. **I will** ______________________________

14 Homegrown Happiness

Extending the Lesson

Using Activity Master 1B: Use the Activity Master "In Search of Happiness." This activity presents two situations for students to consider the source of happiness. In the first, students will evaluate a given situation; for the second, they will examine qualities that contribute to family happiness.

Mime Drama: Enliven the discussion by having students pair up and mime one of the three activity scenarios on the page. Inform them that as with mime, they must communicate without words. Therefore, they need to be overly expressive in their gestures. If appropriate, the class could use this opportunity to play a game of charades, guessing which of the three situations is being mimed.

Activity Master 1A

Name ....

Needs and Happiness

Read the stories and tell what need was met.

1. When Annie was four, she'd look out of her apartment window and imagine a lawn with trees and flowers. Later, she could see only overflowing trash cans and an old brick building marked with graffiti. This morning, Annie looked out with delight: Snow had fallen during the night, putting white hats on the trash cans, dusting the bricks with a powdered-sugar coating.

   What was Annie's need? ______

2. Greg had been giving a lot of extra time and work to math, asking more questions, giving careful answers. Now, warily, he opened his report card and grinned. An A! "Nice going, Greg," said his teacher.

   What was Greg's need? ______

3. Write your story here. Tell what your need was, and how it was filled.

Family Life Grade 8

Activity Master 1B

Name ....

In Search of Happiness

1. First, ask at least two people: If I could have three wishes come true for you, what would your wishes be? Next, list their wishes below. Share them with your classmates, and then decide which are *wants* and which are *needs*. Do you think the wishes would lead to happiness?

2. Look at the italicized qualities that contribute to family happiness. What gets in the way of practicing these at home?

   Why is it sometimes difficult to show *approval*?

   What is most likely to interfere with open *communication*?

   Why is it hard to treat some people with *respect*? Can you show respect without feeling it?

   What kinds of feelings get in the way of *unselfishness*?

Family Life Grade 8

How to Find It How to Use It

Step 1: Click & Select

Go to RCLBFamilyLife.com
Click on the link for activities.
Then select the activity master you need.

Step 2: Print & Copy

Print each activity master in advance.
Then copy enough for everyone in the class.

Step 3: Share & Discuss

Once students have completed the activity, have them share and discuss their responses.

LESSON 2 PLANNER

Goal: To examine the importance of moral formation, especially of our conscience, as necessary for direction in life

Engage
Page 39

Objective
To appreciate the need for direction when feeling lost

Pray
Psalm 119:105, 114, 117, 146–149, 169

Focus
Describe the feeling of being lost.

Discover
Discuss how to best respond to feeling lost.

Teach
Page 40

Objective
To understand how an informed conscience gives direction in life

Focus
Explore the experience of walking blindly and confused.

Explore
Read, discuss and summarize the importance of an informed conscience, grace and counsel in finding good direction in life.
Growing in Virtue: Counsel

Connect
Catholics Believe: Informed conscience
Make an examination of conscience.

Apply
Page 42

Objective
To examine how the gift of counsel guides us in our decisions

Focus
List notable individuals valued for their advice.

Discover
Catholic Family Album: Saint Anne

Integrate
Offer advice in a given situation.

Pray
Prayer to the Holy Spirit for the gift of counsel

Reviewing Unit 1
Summarize and review the content from both lessons.

Vocabulary Preview

Conscience—the inner voice of a human being, within whose heart God's Law is inscribed to judge right from wrong, good from evil

Counsel—Gift of the Holy Spirit in the ability to make right judgments, to choose what is right and good

Free Will—the ability to personally choose for oneself actions with intent and forethought

Morality—the goodness or evil of human acts

Materials Needed

- writing paper
- pens, pencils
- art supplies
- Bible
- Lesson 2 Activity Masters

Call to Prayer

Holy Spirit, you guide us on this journey of life. Help me to share with my students that journey in faith. Help them to see and follow the signs and landmarks of the Father's will. Help me to be a leader by guiding them according to the Son who is the way, the truth and the life. Amen.

Gifts for the Journey

Finding Your Way

After the plane made the emergency landing into the jungle, the survivors decided to group together and figure out what to do next. A storm was approaching, so they decided that they needed to find a safe place to shelter them from the approaching weather.

Gina said, "We don't even know where we are, how are we supposed to find a safe place for shelter?"

People began to argue. "We have no working radio, GPS or other electric devices!" exclaimed Ben. Everyone felt lost.

Then a short stocky man made his way to the front of the group. In broken English he said, "My name is Juan. I lead expeditions through jungles like this. If we can find map or compass, I lead us to safe place."

The group argued some more. They debated letting someone who could barely speak English lead them through this jungle. Another person doubted Juan's ability. Then a few people, who were not arguing found a compass. They approached the group in support of Juan leading them to shelter.

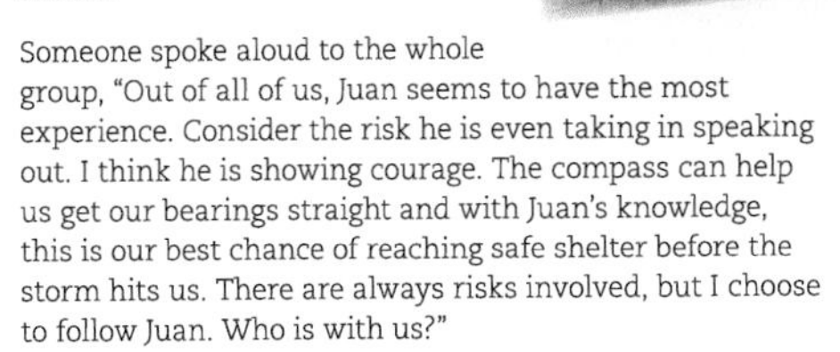

Someone spoke aloud to the whole group, "Out of all of us, Juan seems to have the most experience. Consider the risk he is even taking in speaking out. I think he is showing courage. The compass can help us get our bearings straight and with Juan's knowledge, this is our best chance of reaching safe shelter before the storm hits us. There are always risks involved, but I choose to follow Juan. Who is with us?"

This lesson will help you to:

- **explore** and appreciate the need for direction when feeling lost.
- **understand** how an informed conscience gives direction in life.
- **use** the gift of counsel in making good decisions.

How have you dealt with feeling lost?

Gifts for the Journey 15

Teaching Tip

Basic Rules to Follow: Introduce the students to these basic rules to follow when making decisions:

1. **STOP**—Sit down until you are no longer angry, frustrated, or afraid.
2. **THINK**—What is your situation? Are you in any danger? What resources do you have at hand that you can use to help you find your way?
3. **OBSERVE**—What do you see? Are there any signs that help you recognize where you are? Is there anyone nearby that you can safely ask for help? Are there any signs of potential danger?
4. **DECIDE**—Make a plan for what you will do and then follow it.

Objective

To appreciate the need for direction when feeling lost

Pray

Open the lesson by praying Psalm 119:105, 114, 117, 146–149, 169.

Focus

Have students write a short description of a person feeling lost. Then have them share their descriptions with the class. Write on the board any strong emotions evoked within their descriptions.

Discover

- Read "Finding Your Way." Allow students to ask questions about the reading.
- Have the students identify the various emotions felt by the survivors in the story. Inquire: Which character would you most be like?
- Explain that feeling lost is common. Some decisions deal with life-impacting choices. Feeling lost can disable us from making a good choice.
- Ask: What should you do when you are lost? *(Think, Judge and Act. Don't panic, look for signs to tell you where you are, look for someone you can trust to help you, call for help.)* Who might you trust?
- Discuss with students what gives them direction in their life, especially when they feel lost and alone.

TEACH

Objective

To understand how an informed conscience gives direction in life

Focus

- Have a few volunteers walk blindfolded having just been spun around. Tell them to describe the experience.
- Ask: Why is it disorienting? Explain that without vision and a reference point, it is difficult to move in any direction. Relate the experience to moral decision making. Explain that with clear directions we can still feel lost when we are faced with making a moral decision.

Explore

- Read the Growing in Virtue box. Explain: An informed conscience gives direction making moral decisions, or choices. Share that the gift of counsel helps us make moral decisions.
- Have students quietly read "Checking Your Moral Compass."
- Have students research how a compass works. *(The needle has been magnetized and so it points north.)*
- Discuss with students how following their conscience is like following a compass. Ask: What "magnetizes" your conscience so that it points in the right direction? *(Scripture, Church's moral teachings and advice of parents and teachers)*
- In groups have students identify landmarks and signs that give direction in their life. Share them as a class.

Growing in Virtue

With both an informed conscience and free will, each of us can choose to follow the right path to happiness. The choice can be difficult, but with the aid of grace and the **counsel** of family and friends, we can successfully navigate our way through life.

Checking Your Moral Compass

If you were out in the woods on a camping trip and got lost, you could use a compass to find your way. You could also look for familiar landmarks to help guide you. Regardless of how you find your way, you must first know where you are and where you need to go.

The same is true as you mature and make moral decisions. You might have some tough decisions to face. Some may not be life-threatening, but they are still important. Feeling lost is a common emotion for people at some point in life. Decisions can become more difficult when we face a moral dilemma, that is a decision that has to do with what is right or wrong.

When we feel lost and unsure about what to do, we want to know what is the right thing to do. Sometimes we can see it clearly. Often we need help. We need to find the right person to help us go in the right direction, just like the survivors from the story. For many moral decisions, our parents and the Church can provide the guidance we need.

Think about the times you have felt lost and from whom you sought guidance.

The Church in particular is made up of many amazing people who have joined together over thousands of years searching for what it true, beautiful, and good. The Church has been consistent in her teachings and can be the source for the direction we need. We may experience arguments and doubts, but the Church has been passionate in her pursuit to know what God desires for us. The more we learn about the Church, the more we discover people, just like us, who were lost, but found true happiness in Christ.

The teachings of the Church, your family, and your life experiences all help form your conscience. Your informed conscience helps you to recognize right from wrong, thereby showing a path to happiness. It becomes a frame of reference for making a moral decision. You have the gift of free will to choose to do what is right or what is wrong. Rules

Moral Decisions: Share with the youth that three questions need to be asked to determine the morality of an act: (1) Is the act itself morally good or morally evil? If the act itself is inherently immoral, you have an obligation not to do it. If the act itself is morally good, then proceed. (2) Is my intent to do the inherently morally good act good? If my intent is not good, then I am morally obligated not to do the act. If my intent is good and the act is good, then proceed. If the act is evil but my intention is good, I am obligated not to proceed. In other words, the end does not justify the means. (3) Are the circumstances related to my intent and the act itself morally good or not? If not, then stop; otherwise okay. All three must be good for the act to be a moral (good) act.

like the Ten Commandments, the Golden Rule, the Great Commandment, and the Beatitudes are like maps in life, showing you a path to safe shelter.

Educating and forming your conscience is a life-long task. Reading and studying the teachings of the Church and Sacred Scripture help you, but you still must make decisions. You must practice what you believe. The Holy Spirit can assist you through your parents, teachers, pastor, and other trusted adults. Under the guidance of the Holy Spirit, they can give you counsel or advice on how to navigate your way through life. Yet still the choice is yours. And at some point you too will be asked to give advice, if you haven't already. Making choices that lead you to the fullness of life, love, and happiness is what everyone desires.

Catholics Believe

When confronted with moral decisions, we have a moral obligation to follow our informed conscience. It is to be based on right reason and aligned with truth as willed by God.

"Testing Your Moral Compass"

Everyone needs to test-run their conscience from time to time. Make an examination of conscience to see how you are doing.

Activity

1. *How have I shown respect to others, especially those closest to me?*

___

2. *How have I been kind and helpful to those whom I see daily?*

___

3. *How have my words and actions shown respect for my body and the bodies of others?*

___

4. *How have I respected the truth and been honest in my dealings with others?*

___

5. *How have I dealt with my strong feelings toward others and about life?*

___

6. *How have I kept God first in my life?*

___

Gifts for the Journey 17

Extending the Lesson

Using Activity Master 2A: Use the Activity Master "Laws for a Biosatellite." This activity helps students imagine a situation in which they are compelled to make important decisions based upon ten basic laws that they develop.

When in Doubt: Have students develop scenarios that have a moral decision and discuss as a class. For example, should I go to the party with my friends or stay home to be with my family? If doubt plays a factor, explore the reasons why. If the doubt relates to moral uncertainty, then why risk it if the other option is morally good? A good rule of thumb is "Never act with a doubtful conscience."

- Privately have students evaluate whether their signs are pointing them in a morally good direction that will result in being happy.
- Point out: Conscience is like a compass. A well-informed conscience is set to head to "happiness" just as a regular compass is set to point north.

Connect

- Discuss: Why do we need to properly inform our conscience? Explain that making good moral choices keeps us on the right path to happiness.
- Read the Catholics Believe box. In groups have students identify some guidelines or rules in their family and from the Church that are "to point in the right direction." Write them on the board. (For example, the Ten Commandments, the Beatitudes, the Great Commandment, etc.)
- Have students put together a list of rules of what they should do if they became lost. What rules would they recommend to keep from getting lost? Have the youth relate these rules to making good moral choices.
- Have students complete the activity on the page. If needed, have them finish the activity at home with their family.
- Time permitting, have students discuss why God is important for direction in life.

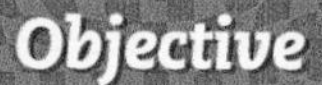

Objective

To examine how the gift of counsel guides us in our decisions

Focus

As a class, develop a list of the people to seek advice from on various topics (for example, fixing a car, biology question, moral decision, peer pressure, an abusive situation). It is important for them to have several trusted adults in their lives with whom they can talk.

Discover

Read, the Catholic Family Album box. Have students imagine the kind of advice Saint Anne might have given to her daughter, Mary. Inquire: Why do you think Saint Anne is so respected in the Church?

Integrate

- Read "Traveling Companions." Respond to any questions students may have about the activity on the page.
- Have students identify qualities of a companion respected for counsel.
- Have students complete the activity on the page.
- Time permitting, have students form an advice panel and respond to one of the scenarios for counsel.

Pray

Pray to the Holy Spirit for the gift of counsel.

Catholic Family Album

Saint Anne is the mother of the Blessed Virgin Mary. Her Hebrew name would be Hannah, meaning, "grace." Tradition holds that Mary's parents were wealthy, devout Jews in their older years when Mary was born. In the early Church, Saint Anne's matriarchal presence had great influence. Imagine what an incredible source for counsel she must have been to her daughter and her grandson, Jesus. By the 13th century her devotion became widespread in the West. Today, there are many shrines dedicated to the grandmother of Jesus Christ, Saint Anne.

Traveling Companions

Family members and friends can be good companions on the journey of life. One way of assisting you is through the gift of counsel. Counsel is one of the seven Gifts of the Holy Spirit. Counsel is the good advice that helps give good direction by helping you see clearly and understand the teachings of Jesus. This wonderful gift of the Spirit is like a moral compass that helps you make choices to follow faithfully the Way of Jesus.

Imagine that the following people are asking you for advice. Use your moral compass to offer some good direction.

1. Your fourth-grade sister has friends who are daring her to shoplift. **I would**
2. Your best friend joined a gang and is pushing you to join too. **I would**
3. You overhear your parents talking about how lonely your grandmother has been since your grandfather passed away. **I would**
4. Think of a real-life situation you know about. What "counsel," or advice, will you give to help someone in that situation?
   Situation
   I will

18 Gifts for the Journey

Extending the Lesson

Using Activity Master 2B: Use the Activity Master "Looking for the Spirit." This activity helps students analyze the meaning of the words and the spirit of God's law in the Ten Commandments.

Gifts of the Spirit: Read Isaiah 11:1–9. Point out that the seven Gifts of the Holy Spirit are: wisdom, understanding, counsel, fortitude, knowledge, piety and fear of the Lord. Explain that wisdom, understanding, counsel and knowledge relate to our mind, or intellect; fortitude, piety and fear of the Lord relate to our will.

ONLINE ACTIVITIES FOR LESSON 2

Activity Master 2A

Name ....

Laws for a Biosatellite

You and your classmates have volunteered to live in space, aboard a biosatellite, for 25 years. It will look like a small community on earth, but will be completely self-sufficient. You'll form a new kind of society, with laws all its own. Write your ideas. Then, work with your fellow pioneers to choose just ten basic laws that you will live by.

Things to think about:

1. Who will make final decisions about the community?
2. How will you ensure equal rights for everyone?
3. How will working days and holidays be scheduled?
4. What laws will be enacted?

Activity Master 2B

Name ....

Looking for the Spirit

Is it possible to obey God's Laws, but not quite live up to their spirit? Look at a few of the Ten Commandments, and see how that might happen.

1. *You shall have no other gods besides me.*

   You probably don't worship a golden calf. But maybe there's something in your life that takes up a lot more time and thought than it should (television, for instance).

   What is that "god" in your life?

2. *Remember to keep holy the Sabbath day.*

   Every Sunday, you go to Mass with your family. Do your activities during the rest of the day also show respect for the Sabbath?

   What basic idea could you carry home from Mass that could make the rest of the day "holy," too?

3. *You shall not steal.*

   You've never robbed a bank or tiptoed away with someone's gold watch. But have you ever taken something valuable away from a person close to you? How could someone's good reputation be stolen?

   How could someone's self-esteem be stolen?

4. *You shall not lie.*

   You've never told a teacher that the dog ate your report. But did you ever change the truth a little?

   You have to admit doing something you regret. Without actually lying, how can you make your story a little less painful?

How to Find It
How to Use It

Step 1: Click & Select

Go to RCLBFamilyLife.com
Click on the link for activities.
Then select the activity master you need.

Step 2: Print & Copy

Print each activity master in advance.
Then copy enough for everyone in the class.

Step 3: Share & Discuss

Once students have completed the activity, have them share and discuss their responses.

REVIEWING UNIT 1

Summary

- Ask the students to read through the Summary section.
- Invite them to ask questions about any points that are not clear to them.
- Make sure to expand on any points that were perhaps touched on only lightly during class time.

Thinking It Through

- Have students answer all three questions on the page.
- Assign each student a number from one through three.
- Have students share with the class their answer to the question that corresponds to their assigned number.

Matching It Up

Use this matching section to help the students be able to identify the appropriate definition or description of a key concept, term or person from the unit.

REVIEWING UNIT 1

Name ....

Summary

Remember what you have learned in each of the lessons in God's Gift of Family.

LESSON 1: Homegrown Happiness

- Everyone has physical, emotional, intellectual, and spiritual needs. These needs are first met in the family.
- God has placed in the human heart the natural desire for happiness. The more we experience gratitude in life, the more we can come to know happiness.
- We often feel our best when we do the work of love in reaching out to those in need.

LESSON 2: Gifts for the Journey

- Feeling lost on our journey to happiness is a common emotion; but God has given us the gift of conscience as our guide.
- With an informed conscience and free will, we can choose to follow the right path to happiness.
- Both the grace of God and the counsel of the Church, family, and friends help us navigate our way through life.

Thinking It Through

1. What do families today need most to be happy?

2. What can families do to help young people make good moral decisions?

3. What are some important ways to form your conscience correctly?

Matching It Up

On each line, write the letter of the description in Column B that best goes with the term in Column A.

A

1. ....D.... Basic needs
2. ....A.... Emotional needs
3. ....B.... Intellectual needs
4. ....E.... Physical needs
5. ....C.... Spiritual needs

B

A. Tony gives Tom, who is learning how to play the piano, plenty of support.
B. Tom practices playing the piano daily.
C. Clare prays while gardening.
D. Families provide food, shelter, security, and care.
E. The Hendersons hike together.

Unit 1 Review 19

Teaching Tip

Parent Letter: Send a letter home to the parents. Tell them to ask their child about what they have learned in unit 1. Encourage the parents to use the Family Time pages at home before and after the unit lessons.

Unit Reviews: These unit review sections do not have to be completed as formal testing or assessments. They are designed to assist students in recalling the essential content of each lesson under their common unit theme. This is an opportunity for either the classroom setting or as a take-home assignment. You can informally assess student progress for each unit as you proceed. Be sure to provide a clear summary of the content in your own words before proceeding to the next unit.

REVIEWING UNIT 1

Name ....

Recalling Key Concepts

Circle the T if the statement is true. Circle the F if the statement is false.

1. The Church is made up of ancient rules that have no relevance to living today. T (F)
2. Happiness is not based on a choice but is something that just happens to you. T (F)
3. When making a decision, I need to worry only about how it makes me feel. T (F)
4. Gratitude is a skill that contributes to one's ability to choose happiness. (T) F
5. Educating and forming my conscience is a life-long task. (T) F

Fill in the missing words in these sentences.

6. **CONSCIENCE** is my inner voice that allows me to make moral decisions; therefore, I have a responsibility to form it according to God's Laws.
7. The **GENEROSITY** of my family and friends contributes to my happiness because of their sharing and my own.
8. **RESPECT** is a sign and attitude that considers one another's needs, feelings, and gifts as important.
9. God gave each of us the gift of **FREE WILL** so that we have the power to choose for ourselves our actions with intent and forethought, be it right or wrong.
10. The skill of acknowledging the importance of someone through honest praise to encourage them to do their best is called **AFFIRMATION**.

Working Together

As a class, make a mural illustrating the Beatitudes. Use photos and words from current events as inspiration for the mural. Form small groups to assign responsibility for each of the eight Beatitudes. If possible, display the mural in public.

20 Unit 1 Review

Teaching Tip

Modeling Respect: Model respect for persons with disabilities by speaking of the person, and if necessary, identifying the disability. For example, rather than saying, "Mary is diabetic and has to have shots." You might say, "Mary has diabetes and has to have shots." Take time to correct students who too casually or insensitively use language when speaking of persons with disabilities. This kind of change in the way we talk can better reflect the truth that a person is not defined by their physical traits.

Recalling Key Concepts

- Use this section to help the students be able to accurately recall the key concepts from the unit.
- For the true and false section, you can have students correct any false statements.
- To help with the fill-in-the-blank section, you might want to provide a word bank on the board.

Working Together

- Choose a project that best fits the needs and abilities of your students, as well as your time schedule.
- Time permitting, have students complete the unit assessment individually or as a class; otherwise, encourage them to complete it at home.

UNIT 2

God's Gift of Self

Background

"[T]rue Christian education of children is not limited to including God among the important things of their [families'] lives, but to put God in the center of this life, so that all the other activities and realities: intelligence, feelings, freedom, work, rest, pain, illness, allergies, material possessions, culture; in a nutshell: everything is molded and ruled by the love to God" (Preparatory Catechesis for the Sixth World Encounter of Families, *Fifth Catechesis 3).*

THE BEGINNING OF WISDOM IS SELF-KNOWLEDGE. In the Christian context, all knowledge must be connected with God. As the above passage notes, God is to be the center of everything. When each person possesses a unique personality, God is to be at the center. It is true that our lives possess a side that rests in mystery, but part of that mystery is the presence of God. So even children should be encouraged to enter in prayerful reflection. In prayer all can center their lives on God.

From any perspective, whether it be the physical, the emotional or the spiritual, we are wondrous mysteries unto ourselves. Our humanity is deeply complex. We spend our entire lifetime on earth asking the important questions, such as: Who am I? Why am I here? Where am I going? In faith, we receive answers to these questions yet there is always more to know. We possess an unquenchable thirst for knowledge, especially knowledge of ourselves.

This thirst is placed in us by God. We seek to know about what makes us tick, about what makes us a person. We learn about our bodies, our emotions, our inner life and our activities. All these areas of life provide us with an endless source of questions. Through the life and teachings of Christ and through his Church, we are given insights into the mystery of our life. We are not left alone to wander; God guides us and walks with us.

Additional Background

Catechism of the Catholic Church:
§§ 1763–1764, 1767, 1769

LEARNING DOES NOT END WITH FORMAL education but continues until the moment of our death. Learning is a lifelong task and adventure. The family should be a place where any question can be asked and any doubts can be explored. Encourage your students to ask questions and seek answers not only in class but, more importantly, at home. Parents are wonderful sources of information and knowledge. They have the rich resource of experience to draw from.

As young people explore their personalities and look to their roots, they can grow in appreciation of themselves as individuals who though unique are much like others. Young people need to explore, accept, be comfortable with and appreciate the reality that God is not quite done with them yet. They are not fully mature and can choose to change and mature as the kind of person God created them to be and to become. They were known before their birth, as the psalmist proclaims in Psalm 139. But they were also created with the gift of free will. This freedom gives them the ability to receive God's graceful presence and grow in surprising, fresh ways.

For Reflection

Read and reflect on the following:

"By free will one shapes one's own life. Human freedom is a force for growth and maturity in truth and goodness" (Catechism of the Catholic Church *1731).*

- When I look at myself, how much of my family's roots and traits do I see in my words and actions? What do I see and hear that is uniquely me?
- What might I do to encourage the young people to grow in self-knowledge and self-acceptance? What might I do to help them grow in their acceptance of others?

Child Safety

One of the developmental tasks of adolescents is learning how to express emotions appropriately. Young teens, stuck in the throes of puberty, often feel frustrated by the changes taking place within them and wonder if anyone will ever consider them attractive and lovable. This may leave them vulnerable to abuse. These lessons will help the students understand that they can take positive steps to manage their feelings appropriately. Such steps will provide support to their self-esteem. A strong and positive self-esteem is one of the greatest defenses against those who seek to take advantage of young people.

Family Time

Family Focus

The family should be a place where any question can be asked and any doubt can be explored. Encourage students to seek answers at home. Parents are wonderful sources of information and knowledge. They have the rich resource of experience to draw from. Welcome the questions and the concerns of your students. Remember, no question is a bad one. Invite parents to use the Parent Connection as a helpful tool in responding to their child's questions.

LESSON 3 PLANNER

Goal: To discover the influences upon a person's personality and how their personality affects their view on life and their decisions

Engage

Page 49

Objective

To examine two major influences in our lives

Family Time

Ensure that each student tears out their Family Time page to complete at home.

Pray

Pray for our families.

Focus

Match photos or images to fellow students.

Discover

Discuss two major influences in life.

Teach

Page 50

Objective

To understand the importance of self-knowledge

Focus

Provoke response with "empty" door prizes.

Explore

Read, discuss and summarize the importance of self-knowledge through an examination of an individual's personality.

Growing in Virtue: Confidence

Catholics Believe: Self-knowledge and freedom

Connect

Write a script of two distinct personalities saving the day.

Apply

Page 52

Objective

To reflect on ways to grow in self-knowledge

Focus:

Catholic Family Album: Saint Albert Chmielowski

Discover

Personal sharing about masks and costumes

Integrate

Self-reflection

Pray

Intercessory prayer

Vocabulary Preview

Confidence—the strength of believing in oneself or developed through accomplishing something worthwhile

Genetic—qualities of living things arising from a common origin and passed from generation to generation through reproduction

Personality—the sum total of all the traits and characteristics that express an individual as distinct from others

Maturity—the state of development that is considered appropriate to a particular intellectual or emotional level or age

Materials Needed

- writing paper
- pens, pencils
- art supplies
- photo of adult relative
- Bible
- Lesson 3 Activity Masters

Call to Prayer

Lord, you gave me roots and wings. Help me to awaken in each of my students the awareness that they too have deep roots and strong wings. Help them to see how you love them as they are. Amen.

Understanding Yourself

Roots and Wings

This lesson will help you to:

- **discover** two major influences in your life.
- **recognize** the importance of self-knowledge.
- **choose** to grow in self-knowledge.

Roots of a large tree are powerful. Unseen beneath the surface, roots carry nourishment from the water and soil to the tree. Roots keep a tree stable in the fiercest winds. From deep roots trees find security. You have roots too. They are found in your family.

Your family provides you nourishment for life. You have become who you are, in part, because of who has helped shape you. You have inherited from your family genetic traits such as curly hair or a tendency to be tall.

Your roots also include environmental influences from where and with whom you live. Shared tastes in food, sports, and hobbies may have been passed along within your family. You have been shaped by many family influences.

How have your roots and wings influenced who you are today?

Watching an eagle fly high in the sky reminds you of the freedom that wings could give you. You may have thought, "If I only had wings with which to fly." In a way, you do have wings. Your parents give you wings by loving you and teaching you about life. Your friends give you wings when they accept you for who you are. Supportive people and positive experiences help you overcome difficulties and therefore help you to fly.

You are not like a tree standing still. God has given you the wings of a unique soul and a free will. You're a unique person. Even if you have an identical twin, your fingerprints, your thoughts, and your choices are yours alone. God's grace gives you the strength to choose what is good and loving, not what is sinful and evil. With roots and wings, you can freely discover yourself soaring to the heights of finding life and love.

Teaching Tip

Roots Give Confidence: Self-esteem, how one feels about one's self, is based upon three aspects: (1) feeling loved, (2) feeling valued and (3) having self-confidence. Confidence comes from being rooted in one's faith and family values. Children with low self-esteem often blame themselves when bad things happen. They are also easy targets for child abusers. Help your students grow in confidence. Encourage them to use their God-given gifts to bravely attempt new challenges. Let them know that you believe that they can succeed. Help them develop a healthy sense of pride in their accomplishments. When students try and fail, congratulate their attempt and help them to see how to improve their efforts.

Objective

To examine two major influences in our lives

Pray

Open the lesson with a prayer for our families.

Focus

Ask students in advance to bring in an unlabeled photo of an adult relative. Post them by number and have students match students to adults. An alternative is to use images of objects that symbolize or best represent each student.

Discover

- Read "Roots and Wings." Allow students to ask questions about the reading.
- Draw on the board a large tree with roots. Then have them label the roots with qualities that are genetic, environmental or learned. Talk about the stability a tree's roots provide. In what ways do their family's faith and values provide them with stability?
- Above and around the tree have students write the names of people who help them become confident and strong.
- Time permitting, have students discuss favorite family influences, such as food, games, music, traditions, etc. Have students explain how these are passed on from one generation to the next.

TEACH

Objective

To understand the importance of self-knowledge

Focus

- Before class, randomly tape a note that says "Winner" under the seat of five desks.
- Tell students that you are awarding five door prizes. Have them look under their desk seats. Winners should come forward to receive their prize.
- Congratulate the winners, but refrain from any further comments about it and have the students return to their seats.

Explore

- Have students quietly read the text on the page. Allow time for students to react or ask questions.
- Invite students to define what personality is and isn't.
- Refer to the opening activity and ask students to recall how the winners responded to the lack of prizes. Note that their responses gave a clue to their personality through their way of responding.
- Ask students to define a "winning" personality. What would be its attributes? How could they have such a personality?
- Read the Growing in Virtue box. Explain: Others can help you better understand yourself, especially friends.

Growing in Virtue

Confidence is about standing tall and reaching high. The more you understand yourself and value the person God created you to be, the more confidence you will have in yourself and in life.

What a Personality!

One of the most important things you will learn as you mature is that every human being is an individual. Each person thinks, acts, and feels differently from the way others do. People have personal tastes, and may react differently to the same event.

Each person has an individual personality. Personality arises from the sum total of all the traits and characteristics that express who a person is. When you describe someone as shy or outgoing, optimistic or pessimistic, practical or a daydreamer, you are describing aspects of their personality.

Personality is more than just the emotion or feeling of the moment. Anger, joy, fear, and other emotions come and go, but your personality stays with you. Your personality influences the way you experience and handle emotions. For example, a shy person might feel joy as a quiet inner glow expressed with a smile. An outgoing person, on the other hand, might express joy as an explosion while shouting with delight. Your personality creates the stage on which all your emotions are played out.

Think about some of your personality traits and how you express them.

Taking Time

Though our personality offers some real clues toward our growing in self-knowledge and relationships, our personality is very complex and not easily charted. Because you are created in God's image and likeness, you are a wonderful mystery unfolding with endless possibilities. Knowing and naming your personality traits and growing in self-knowledge takes time.

People grow and change, develop and make choices. A pessimist may become an optimist. A daydreamer may learn the practical skills to make their dreams come true. A shy person may become someone who loves the spotlight. Your life can and will develop and change; it is not set in stone.

24 Understanding Yourself

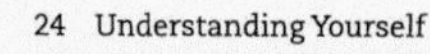

Teaching Tip

Understanding Personality: Some scientists think that the primary source of social behavior could be heredity. Others think that social behaviors are primarily learned in the enculturation process. Most social scientists think both are needed. As a teacher, it is important that you understand the personalities of your students. Some will be moody, some happy, some optimists, some pessimists; all are in development and influenced by how others, including you, treat them. Don't let their personalities determine your behavior. Remember that each child is made in God's image and likeness. Be sure to treat each child with dignity and respect, and model for them Christian love and understanding.

Taking time to get to know your own personality will help you grow in confidence and adjust more easily to the changes of puberty. Taking this time will help you make the best use of your strengths and overcome your weaknesses.

Confidence in who you are develops from understanding yourself. Knowing more about your personality will build the inner strength to achieve success. Confidence is about standing tall and reaching high. Your roots ground you in the truth of who are you, while your wings enable you to exceed expectations.

Taking time to understand other people's personalities is also key to confidently building and maintaining friendships and other relationships. Recognizing and accepting the fact that people are unique individuals can help you appreciate the gifts they can offer. Having respect for others is a sign of maturity—and also of self-confidence.

In God's plan for your life, your personality is not a lock, but a key. It is a key to understanding yourself and others.

Catholics Believe

Our soul is the innermost part of who we are. It is how God has created us in his image and likeness. Each human soul is unique, individual, and immortal, immediately created by God. Our soul gives us the power of self-knowledge and freedom.

"Dynamic Duo"

Work with a partner to write a script in which you and your partner are superheroes saving the day. One of you is cautious and the other is daring. Then act out the script for the whole group.

Extending the Lesson

Using Activity Master 3A: Use the Activity Master "The Shape of You." This activity helps students further identify ways in which their personality is influenced by their foundation found in the roots of their inherited traits and their inspiration discovered in the wings of their environmental influences.

Recognizing Others: Have students design and give Roots and Wings awards to members of their family and friends who have nurtured them and helped them build confidence in themselves. Invite a student or group of students to design the award for use in this activity. Encourage them to present the award in a public way to give greater honor to that person.

TEACH

- Have each student write their name and one quirky fact about themselves on a slip of paper.
- Gather the slips and read aloud each fact as a question, for example, Who can make bread? Have students guess which of their fellow students has this talent.
- As a private activity, ask students to describe their personality, what they like about it and what they would like to change. Help them to understand that their personality doesn't determine them, but that they can determine their personalities. They can change their personality over time, if they choose.
- Remind students that personality is neither good nor bad; people are good because everyone is created in God's image and likeness. And God loves you always.
- Explain that despite our personalities being complex, each of us is capable of self knowledge.
- Read the Catholics Believe box.

Connect

- Pair up students and have them describe each other's personality in three words.
- Have students complete the activity on the page. If needed, have them finish the activity at home with their family.
- Time permitting, have students discuss how their personality has changed as they have matured.

APPLY

Objective

To reflect on ways to grow in self-knowledge

Focus

Read the Catholic Family Album box. Explain that Saint Albert was a role model for Saint John Paul II. Inquire: Who has dressed up as a Saint in costume? Have student explain why they chose that person. How is that Saint a role model for you and others today?

Discover

Invite students to share their experiences of masks. Display images of masks from theater, Halloween, Mardi Gras, etc. Discuss how masks help us take on a personality.

Integrate

- Read "Strictly Personal." Respond to any questions students may have about the activity on the page.
- Have students complete the activity on the page.
- Time permitting, have students discuss the positive and negative aspects of wearing a mask.

Pray

Pray for the intercession of the students' favorite Saints.

Catholic Family Album

Saint Albert Chmielowski was born in 1845 to a wealthy family living in Poland. Adam, his birth name, was interested in politics and art, but also felt called to help those in serious need. Eventually he became a Franciscan, taking the name of Albert, and formed a group who provided food and shelter for the poor and homeless. Albert made a difference in the lives of the people of his time. More than a century later, Karol Wojtyla (Saint John Paul II) was highly influenced by Saint Albert and even wrote a play about him. The Pope said that he found great spiritual encouragement from Saint Albert.

Strictly Personal

The words *personal* and *personality* come from the Greek word *persona*, which is the name for the large masks worn by actors in ancient Greek theater. These "persona," or masks, were structured to amplify the actor's voice and to exaggerate facial expressions. The masks enabled the actor to be heard and seen from a distance. In the same way, your personality projects who you are, what you believe in and what you consider important.

Reflect on the questions below. The questions are meant to help you discover how your personality reflects who you are. Then write the questions and your answers in a notebook or journal. Your answers are meant to be strictly personal—but you may choose to share them with a family member or friend.

Make a commitment to do the exercise often to grow in self-knowledge and self-confidence.

What do I like best about myself?
Which family members am I most like?
What would I most like to change about myself?
What family rule helps me the most right now?

What is my deepest hope?
Why is my Catholic faith important to me?
Where do I find God?

Who are some people I most admire?
How important are my friends to me? Why?
How do I spend most of my free time?

What do I see myself doing in five years? In twenty-five?
What difference is my life making in the life of others?
What difference will my life make in the world?

26 Understanding Yourself

Extending the Lesson

Using Activity Master 3B: Use the Activity Master "Beware of Labels." This activity helps students discuss and debate the positive and negative aspects of stereotyping people with labels and why stereotyping results in inaccurate or improper judgments.

Art Activity: Discuss ahead of time with the art teacher or go online to learn how to make paper mache. Have students create a paper-mache mask that reflects the most positive and dominant personality traits they see in themselves. Discuss how color can symbolize certain attributes, for example, red could give a sense of strength while blue gives a sense of calmness.

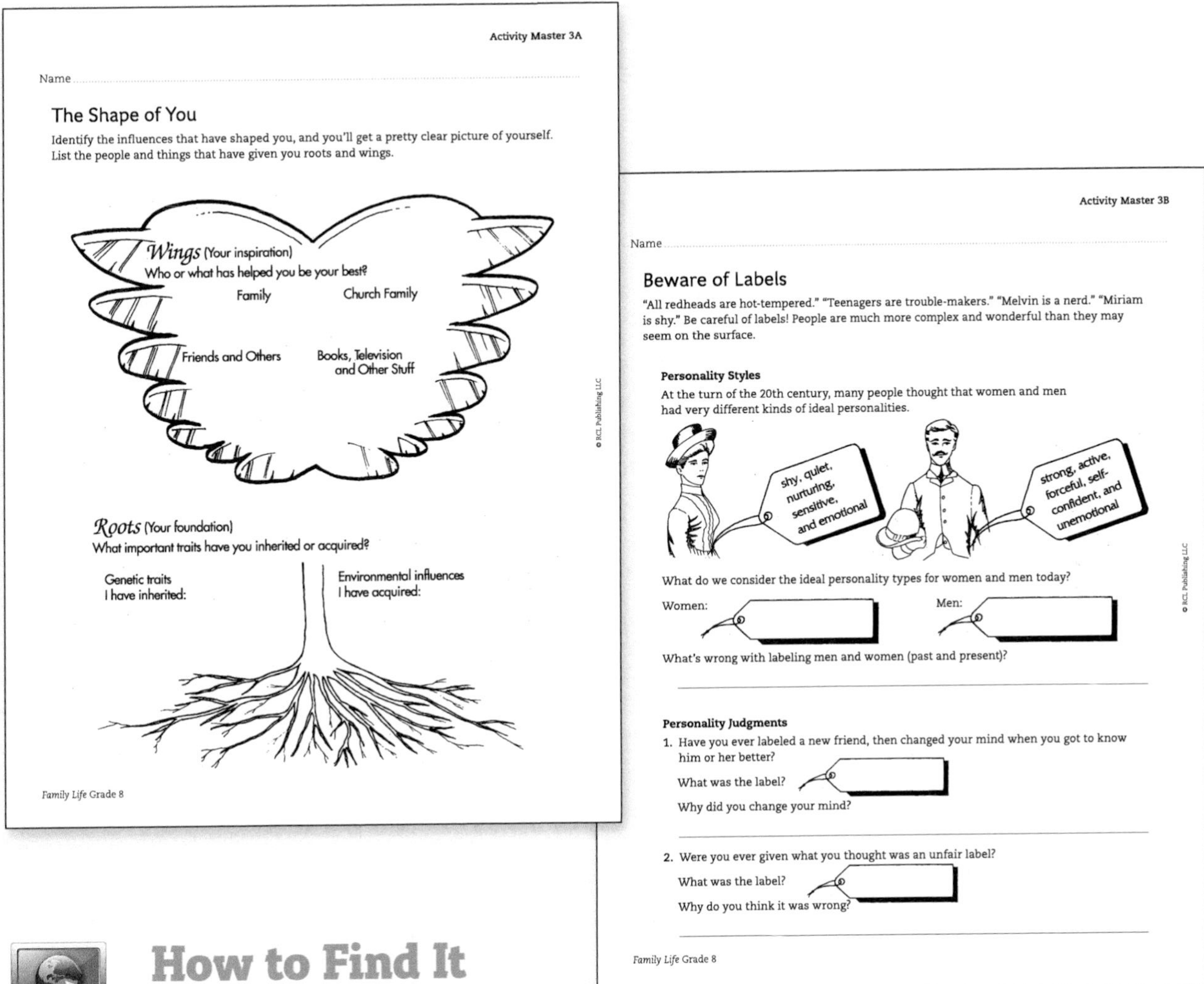

Activity Master 3A

Name

The Shape of You

Identify the influences that have shaped you, and you'll get a pretty clear picture of yourself. List the people and things that have given you roots and wings.

Wings (Your inspiration)
Who or what has helped you be your best?
Family
Church Family
Friends and Others
Books, Television and Other Stuff

Roots (Your foundation)
What important traits have you inherited or acquired?
Genetic traits I have inherited:
Environmental influences I have acquired:

Family Life Grade 8

© RCL Publishing LLC

Activity Master 3B

Name

Beware of Labels

"All redheads are hot-tempered." "Teenagers are trouble-makers." "Melvin is a nerd." "Miriam is shy." Be careful of labels! People are much more complex and wonderful than they may seem on the surface.

Personality Styles

At the turn of the 20th century, many people thought that women and men had very different kinds of ideal personalities.

shy, quiet, nurturing, sensitive, and emotional

strong, active, forceful, self-confident, and unemotional

What do we consider the ideal personality types for women and men today?

Women:
Men:

What's wrong with labeling men and women (past and present)?

Personality Judgments

1. Have you ever labeled a new friend, then changed your mind when you got to know him or her better?
What was the label?
Why did you change your mind?

2. Were you ever given what you thought was an unfair label?
What was the label?
Why do you think it was wrong?

Family Life Grade 8

© RCL Publishing LLC

How to Find It
How to Use It

Step 1: Click & Select

Go to RCLBFamilyLife.com
Click on the link for activities.
Then select the activity master you need.

Step 2: Print & Copy

Print each activity master in advance.
Then copy enough for everyone in the class.

Step 3: Share & Discuss

Once students have completed the activity, have them share and discuss their responses.

LESSON 4 PLANNER

Goal: To examine the importance of our emotions and to develop the skills and techniques in handling them properly and morally

Engage

Page 55

Objective

To examine how emotions affect our decisions

Pray

Prayer of thanksgiving

Focus

Match emotions and colors.

Discover

Discuss how emotions send us messages.

Teach

Page 56

Objective

To understand how to handle strong emotions in virtuous ways

Focus

Share personal experiences of strong emotions.

Explore

Read, discuss and summarize the importance of virtuous living especially in responding to strong emotions in a healthy way.

Growing in Virtue: Valor

Catholics Believe: Hope

Connect

Create a billboard about needed virtues for teens.

Apply

Page 58

Objective

To identify ways to experience joy through good choices

Focus

Catholic Family Album: Saint Joan of Arc

Discover

Evaluate well-known individuals as positive and negative role models.

Integrate

Create and recognize moments of joy.

Pray

Intercessory prayer

Reviewing Unit 2

Summarize and review the content from both lessons.

Vocabulary Preview

Emotions—feelings that you experience in response to everything that affects you

Hope—Theological Virtue by which we desire and expect from God both happiness and the grace we need to attain it

Valor—the ability to face challenges in life with the strength of mind, will and spirit

Materials Needed

- writing paper
- pens, pencils
- art supplies
- slips of paper
- Bible
- Lesson 4 Activity Masters

Call to Prayer

O Holy Spirit, come help us. Remind me that emotions are God-given resources for life. Guide me in leading my students toward virtue in their life. Inspire us all to live as people filled with your love and truth. Amen.

Emotions

The Good, the Bad, the Ugly

We all have emotions and express them in our own ways. Take a moment and think of the emotions you have felt today. Then think about the emotions others have expressed. Image what it would be like to be at the Super Bowl when the winning touchdown was scored in overtime and there was absolutely no emotion felt and expressed by the crowd. Everyone just stood up, folded up their seat, and left. A world without emotions would be a pretty dull place.

This lesson will help you to:

- **explore** the role emotions play in making decisions.
- **understand** how to direct strong emotions in virtuous ways.
- **identify** and choose ways to experience joy through good choices.

Emotions are simply part of being human. Emotions send you important messages related to your well-being. They are feelings you experience in response to everything that affects you. They can vary in intensity and are transitory. Some feelings, such as excitement, relief, hopefulness, and attraction, can positively affect us. Other feelings, such as loneliness, grief, and jealousy can affect us negatively. Both positive and negative emotions are important.

Whether positive or negative, emotions are neither right nor wrong. They are neither morally good nor bad in themselves. However, what you choose to do with your emotions is a different matter altogether. How you choose to act on your feelings can be morally good or bad. Sorting this out can be challenging because your emotions can make choosing the right thing to do difficult. Understanding your emotions and making choices based on what Jesus teaches us through the Church can lead you to decisions that will enrich rather than harm your life.

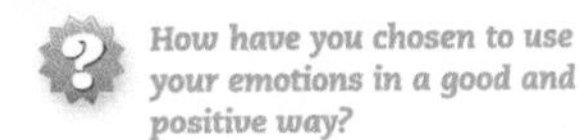

How have you chosen to use your emotions in a good and positive way?

The important thing to remember is that you have choices. Your emotions cannot make you do anything. That is because God gave you free will. Along with all your emotions, God also created you with an intellect for knowing, a conscience for deciding, and a free will for choosing. With the use of reason and the aid of God's grace, you can choose to use your emotions in a good and positive way as Jesus himself did.

Emotions 27

Teaching Tip

Engaging Students: Emotions are part of being human. While all people have emotions, the intensity of those emotions will differ among people. People can have different emotions to the same event. Some people might be angry while others are motivated. Therefore, it is important that you know how your students respond to challenges and disappointments. Remember that your students all have their own emotional and psychological needs. If these needs are not met, they are likely to become frustrated and act out in some way. Youth like to be challenged with issues they see relevant to their lives. Varying your teaching approaches and using different types of activities can help to engage students.

ENGAGE

Objective

To examine how emotions affect our decisions

Pray

Open the lesson with a prayer thanking God for creating us as we are.

Focus

Have students list emotions and a corresponding color on the board; for example, envious—green, angry—red.

Discover

- Read "The Good, the Bad, the Ugly." Allow students to ask questions about the reading.
- Call on five students to place a (+) next to the emotions listed on the board they regard as positive. Then have five others place a (-) next to those they regard as negative. Expect some disagreements.
- Discuss how our emotions send us messages. Have students give an example of the message a negative emotion might be giving; for example, fear might be telling us to be cautious.
- Ask: How would you respond to someone who said people are not responsible for their actions? Reinforce that emotions in themselves are neither good nor bad. How we use or express our feelings is what makes our words and actions good or evil, virtuous or sinful.

TEACH

Objective

To understand how to handle strong emotions in virtuous ways

Focus

- Invite students to share a personal experience where they or another person seemed to be carried away with emotion. For example, close sports events, major life event, presence of a celebrity, etc.
- Have the youth identify and assess the intensity of the emotion and how it was expressed. Then have them describe how the situation ended.

Explore

- Have students quietly read the text on the page. As a class read it aloud, pause for students to react or ask questions.
- Inquire: What dragons have they ever encountered?
- Read the Growing in Virtue box. Explain that the virtue of valor comes from other virtues like patience, hope and chastity.
- Place students in groups explaining that each group is to report back to the class what they discussed. Assign each group one of the strong emotions: anger, sadness, attraction. Have each group reread those sections, define the emotion and give examples of its expression.

Growing in Virtue

The person who has been able to face the challenges of anger, sadness, and attraction with patience, hope, and chastity has shown great **valor** in life. This makes such a person a hero who turns problems into possibilities.

Problems and Possibilities

Your teen years are a lot like those ancient legends in which the hero faced tests and dangers in order to achieve victory. Like a hero, you have been given special gifts to help you turn problems into possibilities.

Valor is the defining trait of a hero. It is the virtuous ability to face challenges in life with the strength of mind, will, and spirit. Valor reflects the Cardinal Virtue of fortitude, and can move you to make the right choice even when emotional barriers stand in the way.

Ancient map makers once marked especially dangerous or unknown areas of the world with the words, "Here be dragons." On your journey through adolescence there are three particular emotions that signal a similar warning: anger, sadness, and attraction. With valor you can face the challenges these emotions will present to you and also conquer the "dragons" they may be.

Think about how you deal with anger, sadness, and attraction.

Anger, Sadness, and Attraction

You may already have noticed that during this stage of your life you are more easily angered at times. Part of the reason for this increase in anger is physical. Your body is flooded with strong hormones that give you a lot of energy. Feeling angry at this time in your life is quite natural. For some people the anger comes as a sudden flare up. For others it is a vague sense of being irritated. Sometimes you might feel like you are about to explode.

Three headed Dragon spitting fire by German School (19th century)

The virtue of patience can help you properly deal with your anger. When you feel anger rising within you, pause and slow down your breathing. You can also exercise or do something relaxing, such as listening to music. If you feel angry during a conversation, you can say "I'm really feeling angry right now." This will

28 Emotions

Teaching Tip

Dealing with Anger: Anger is a normal emotion for young teens. There are signs at the onset of anger. For example, the person will start to breathe faster and their face may turn red. Their body might stiffen and their responses become sharp. Here are some steps you can take to help deal with anger:

- Call a time-out.
- Invite the student to talk about the cause of their feeling.
- Have the student take deep breaths to relax and to think about what caused the anger.

Have the student work on something different that is fun for them to redirect their attention off their anger.

give others a chance to deal with you on an honest level. Whatever you do, always be patient with yourself; you're learning along the way.

Sadness is another strong emotion young people experience during puberty. Crying, which can be by-product of stirred-up hormones, may accompany sadness. You may sense gloomy moods or feel great loneliness. The signal of these down moods may be to move you toward the comfort of family and friends. The virtue of hope helps you face sad and troubling times, knowing and trusting that God is always there for you.

Feelings of sexual attraction can also increase during puberty. These feelings are normal. These feelings are a positive sign that men and women are meant to carry out together God's plan for love and new life. Sexual emotions are among some of the most powerful. The virtue of chastity is so important in helping you to live God's gift of love in ways appropriate for your age. It will help you channel the energy of sexual attraction into positive areas, such as developing real friendships and exploring creative talents.

Catholics Believe

The Theological Virtue of hope opens up the heart to desire and expect the happiness promised by God. Hope prepares us to be with God and sustains us until we are with him. The person filled with hope is preserved from selfishness and is moved to do the work of charity (see *Catechism of the Catholic Church* 1818).

"Shield of Valor"

Choose one of the three virtues discussed in this section. Work with a partner or by yourself and create a billboard promoting to young teens the value of living this virtue.

Activity

Emotions 29

- Explain to students that people's emotions are often linked to their self-esteem. If they feel good about themselves, their emotions are positive; but if they feel bad, their emotions turn negative.
- Ask: "What does 'playing with my emotions' mean?" How might a person take advantage of a person's emotions? How can a person guard themselves from another person in this situation?

- Read the Catholics Believe box. Explain that hope is a Theological Virtue as are faith and charity.
- Then have each group give an example of the related virtues of patience, hope and chastity.
- Have each group report to the class on what they discussed.

Connect

- Have students individually complete the activity on the page. If needed, have them finish the activity at home with their family. They can choose the virtue they think is most needed in their class or in the school or for their age group.
- Time permitting, have students display their billboards around the room or in the halls.

Extending the Lesson

Using Activity Master 4A: Use the Activity Master "Emotions and Choices." This activity helps students further examine the choices they have in dealing with or handling a strong emotion. The emotions of anger, sadness, fear and pleasure are identified.

Old World Research: Gather medieval maps or images from the Internet or from the library. Show the students how the people at that time depicted the unknown and the dangerous. Discuss the common legends of various heroes and heroines, such as Saint George. Entertain a discussion about the "dragons" of today that brave men and women are now called to slay.

APPLY

Objective

To identify ways to experience joy through good choices

Focus

Read, the Catholic Family Album box. Ask: How was Saint Joan of Arc a Christian hero? *(She fought the dragon that was attempting to break her faith in Christ.)*

Discover

Invite students to cite modern day examples of Saints and other role models in their life. Contrast them with celebrities who show a lack of valor in living the Christian life. Discuss the kinds of lives that result.

Integrate

- Read "Handling Your Emotions." Respond to any questions students may have about the activity on the page.
- Have students complete the activity on the page.
- Time permitting, have students discuss the positive and negative influences in life and how they can surround themselves with more positive than negative.

Pray

Pray for the intercession of the students' patron Saints.

Catholic Family Album

Saint Joan of Arc felt called by God to help restore the rightful king of France, King Charles VII, to the throne. This calling began in 1425 when she was thirteen. It was at that time she began to receive "counsel" or messages from Saints. Later they became visions, some being of Saint Michael the Archangel. While many were skeptical of Joan and her mission, she faced the challenges of her calling with valor. She helped restore Charles as king. Yet Joan of Arc was later betrayed, imprisoned and executed. In 1920 Pope Benedict XV canonized Joan of Arc, and she remains a model of valor for Christians.

Handling Your Emotions

As you grow in wisdom, you will learn that the responses you make to emotional impulses will have a huge effect or consequences in your life. When you respond to your emotions in positive ways, they make you stronger and more confident in yourself.

Learning to manage your emotions takes practice. When you and your friends are trying to figure out what to do, choose an activity that improves your mood by giving you joy. Using the illustration below, write on each slip of paper an activity that might improve your mood. For example, it might include music, hobby, a sport, or game. Then recall these activities when you realize that you need to help bring joy back into your life.

Extending the Lesson

Using Activity Master 4B: Use the Activity Master "Safety Valves." This activity helps students examine how to handle the pressure felt from strong emotions given in the two scenarios.

Course of Action: Have students describe an emotional situation that they have recently experienced. Perhaps they have felt envious of trendy apparel that they cannot afford and have been tempted to shoplift something or steal money. Then have them discuss the experience by responding to the following: (1) What was your emotion? (2) What was your response to the emotion? (3) What was the right or proper course of action?

ONLINE ACTIVITIES FOR LESSON 4

Activity Master 4A

Name ....

Emotions and Choices

You're not a slave to your emotions; you can decide how to use them. In each section, write a positive and a negative way you might deal with each emotion.

Emotion	Action
Anger at your soccer team for losing an important game.	Positive: Negative:
Sadness about a friend injured by a drunk driver.	Positive: Negative:
Fear of giving an important oral report.	Positive: Negative:
Pleasure at being admired for your musical talent.	Positive: Negative:

Activity Master 4B

Name ....

Safety Valves

If you sealed a lid on a pot of water, and then started it boiling, you'd produce big trouble. If you try to seal off your emotions, you can end up with the same effect. The secret is to drain off that explosive energy. Prepare your safety valves now!

1. You overslept and missed breakfast. You left your backpack on the bus. You saw the special person in your life with someone else. You come home, and your mom says, "I need you to run an errand for me, now." The dog growls at you; little brother sticks out his tongue.

   What are some possible safety valves you can use?

   ____

   ____

   ____

   ____

   ____

   ____

2. Amazing! You and this classmate of the opposite sex had barely noticed each other before. At first, just exchanging a long look was exciting, and even holding hands created electric sparks. Now you're spending more time together, and each time, you want to be closer. You don't want to hurt anyone's feelings, but it's getting a little scary. How can you help yourself and each other?

   What are some possible safety valves you can use?

   ____

   ____

   ____

   ____

   ____

   ____

How to Find It
How to Use It

Step 1: Click & Select

Go to RCLBFamilyLife.com
Click on the link for activities.
Then select the activity master you need.

Step 2: Print & Copy

Print each activity master in advance.
Then copy enough for everyone in the class.

Step 3: Share & Discuss

Once students have completed the activity,
have them share and discuss their responses.

Summary

- Ask the students to read through the Summary section.
- Invite them to ask questions about any points that are not clear to them.
- Make sure to expand on any points that were perhaps touched on only lightly during class time.

Thinking It Through

- Have students answer all three questions on the page.
- Assign each student a number from one through three.
- Have students share with the class their answer to the question that corresponds to their assigned number.

Matching It Up

Use this matching section to help the students identify the appropriate definition or description of a key concept, term or person from the unit.

REVIEWING UNIT 2

Name ....

Summary

Remember what you have learned in each of the lessons in God's Gift of Self.

LESSON 3: Understanding Yourself

- Each person is created with a soul, an intellect, and free will. Inherited traits and environmental influences contribute to the person you are.
- Self-knowledge is important in understanding God's plan for your life.
- Understanding your personality will help you have greater self-confidence and mature in your relationships with others.

LESSON 4: Emotions

- Emotions are natural responses to everything that affects a person. How you act on your emotions can be right or wrong.
- The Theological Virtue of hope opens up a person's heart to desire and expect the happiness God promises.
- Being able to face challenges in life with valor enables a person to turn problems into possibilities.

Thinking It Through

1. How can you work to overcome negative influences or obstacles?

2. How is self-control a sign of maturity?

3. Why is understanding your emotions important in relating with others and respecting yourself?

Matching It Up

On each line, write the letter of the description in Column B that best goes with the term in Column A.

A

1. ....D.... Chastity
2. ....C.... Confidence
3. ....E.... Hope
4. ....A.... Patience
5. ....B.... Valor

B

A. I'm feeling really angry, so I need to take a break.
B. Despite the difficulties, I am able to face this challenge.
C. I know that I can do this.
D. I want to get to know you as a friend.
E. With God's grace, I can help you.

Unit 2 Review 31

REVIEWING UNIT 2

Name ....

Recalling Key Concepts

Circle the T if the statement is true. Circle the F if the statement is false.

1. Some emotions are good, while others are bad. T (F)
2. All people think, act, and feel the same. T (F)
3. Emotions are the feelings that human beings experience in response to everything that affects them. (T) F
4. Personality is just the typical personal emotional response to a given moment. T (F)
5. The word *persona* refers to the name for the large masks worn by actors in theater. (T) F

Fill in the missing words in these sentences.

6. **INHERITED** traits from your family, such as curly hair or a tendency to be tall, are genetic.
7. Having **RESPECT** for yourself and others is a sign of maturity.
8. **CHASTITY** is an important virtue that helps you to live God's gift of love in ways appropriate for your age.
9. Ancient map makers once marked especially dangerous or unknown areas with the words, "Here be **DRAGONS**."
10. Shy, outgoing, and optimistic are all examples of **PERSONALITY** traits.

Working Together

In small groups, create a cheer, rap, poem, or song about handling difficult emotions. After you have finished writing it, hold a class talent show and present your creations to one another.

32 Unit 2 Review

Teaching Tip

Review Gifts of the Holy Spirit: Read Isaiah 11:1–9. Point out that the seven Gifts of the Holy Spirit are: wisdom, understanding, counsel, fortitude, knowledge, piety and fear of the Lord. Explain that wisdom, understanding, counsel and knowledge relate to our mind, or intellect; fortitude, piety and fear of the Lord relate to our will. Have students identify one example from their daily life for each of the seven gifts.

REVIEWING UNIT 2

Recalling Key Concepts

- Use this section to help the students be able to accurately recall the key concepts from the unit.
- For the true and false section, you can have students correct any false statements.
- To help with the fill-in-the-blank section, you might want to provide a word bank on the board.

Working Together

- Choose a project that best fits the needs and abilities of your students, as well as your time schedule.
- Time permitting, have students complete the unit assessment individually or as a class; otherwise, encourage them to complete it at home.

UNIT 3

God's Gift of Life

Background

*"[T]he Church firmly believes that human life, even if weak and suffering, is always a splendid gift of God's goodness. Against the pessimism and selfishness which cast a shadow over the world, the Church stands for life: in each human life she sees the splendor of that 'Yes,' that 'Amen,' who is Christ Himself. To the 'No' which assails and afflicts the world, she replies with this living 'Yes,' thus defending the human person and the world from all who plot against and harm life" (*Familiaris Consortio *30).*

GOD IS THE CREATOR OF LIFE AND SUSTAINS LIFE. God desires that all live and have life in its fullest through the power of his love. Life is a gift. As creatures of God, we do not have the right to take or destroy human life. That has been and is the constant teaching of the Church. Indifference to human life is a sure sign of a godless perspective. We are to preserve and enhance life whenever possible.

Sadly we have been living through a time, where in many places and among many individuals, human life is not valued as a sacred gift. Young people cannot help but be aware of the realities of violence, even as they study the value of life. Outside of class (and perhaps in school in the form of bullying), some of them have probably experienced real-life violence.

The Church has responded to this culture of violence by asserting over and over again that "Human life is sacred because from its beginning it involves the creative action of God and it remains forever in a special relationship with the Creator, who is its sole end. God alone is the Lord of life from its beginning until its end" (*Donum Vitae* 5). In recent years the Church has continuously reasserted this truth by speaking out against abortion, infanticide, murder, torture, capital punishment, unjust wars, euthanasia and any act that attacks the sacredness of human life. Sometimes this stand is not popular but it is a value that the Church and all her members must abide in.

THE CATHOLIC CHURCH CONSISTENTLY PROMOTES a culture of life. Catholics are called to be pro-life with consistency and comprehensiveness. We cannot pick and choose which issue of life to be for or against. Again God alone is the author of human life and he alone is Lord. Help your students see practical ways that they can take a stand with the Church for life.

Given the ambivalence of many in today's culture on life issues, many students may not have received with clarity all that it means to support human life. They may not recognize that certain common practices, such as smoking tobacco, taking illicit drugs or drinking alcohol before one is of age are expressions of being anti-life. Taking good care of oneself is part of being pro-life. Helping others to do the same expresses similar respect for life.

Additional Background

Catechism of the Catholic Church: §§ 1706, 2258–2283, 2319, 2322, 2348–2350

There are many reports of anti-life events reported on the news each day. Discuss appropriately these happenings with your students. What information they receive from their peers may not be reliable or even correct. Ensure that your students know the challenges of our time.

For Reflection

Read and reflect on the following:

"Life and physical health are precious gifts entrusted to us by God. We must take reasonable care of them, taking into account the needs of others and the common good" (Catechism of the Catholic Church *2288).*

- How clearly do my actions show that I value my life as a sacred gift from God?
- What might I do to help the young people strengthen their resolve to care for their well-being and avoid self-destructive choices?

Child Safety

The two lessons in this unit focus on protecting the dignity of human life. Lesson 5 addresses the various forms of violence that are experienced in the world, including child abuse. Lesson 6 looks at the ways that people may harm themselves. All violence and self-abusive behavior wound human dignity and are violations of God's law of love. Be knowledgeable about the parish's or school's policies regarding child safety.

Family Time

Family Focus

There are many stories of anti-life events reported on the news each day. Discuss these happenings with the students. What information they receive from their peers may not be reliable or even correct. Ensure that students know the challenges of our time. There are many conflicting views floating around these days. Even a small amount of solid Christian understanding of life will go a long way. Invite parents to review the Family Time pages at home with their child to discuss and learn with clarity the gift of life.

LESSON 5 PLANNER

Goal: To understand the major threats to human life that plague society in order to evaluate attitudes towards life and the dignity of the human person

Engage
Page 65

Objective
To examine how society views the value of human life

Family Time
Ensure that each student tears out their Family Time page to complete at home.

Pray
Prayer for life

Focus
Define *violence* and *sacred.*

Discover
Discuss current news items in light of society's view of human life.

Teach
Page 66

Objective
To identify some major threats to human life

Focus
Survey students' attitudes toward "life issues."

Explore
Read, discuss and summarize the importance of dignity of the human person and how it is violated by grave acts of violence.
Catholics Believe: Human life is sacred.
Growing in Virtue: Respect

Connect
List practical ways to stand against threats to human life.

Apply
Page 68

Objective
To evaluate attitudes in order to promote change with action

Focus
Catholic Family Album: Cyber Bridges

Discover
Matthew 15:10–20

Integrate
Personal assessment

Pray
Prayer for respect for all life

Vocabulary Preview

Abortion—the direct killing of the unborn human person growing inside the womb of the mother; direct abortion

Eugenics—the manipulation of human mating and reproduction in order to "enhance" the human race by eliminating certain "undesirable" attributes

Euthanasia—the deliberate killing of a person who is elderly, severely disabled or suffering from serious or terminal illness

Murder—the direct and intentional killing of an innocent person

Materials Needed

- writing paper
- pens, pencils
- art supplies
- Bible
- online news agencies
- Lesson 5 Activity Masters

Call to Prayer

Praise you God, our Creator! You are the author of life. Thank you for giving me life. Show me how to share my joy in life with my students. Let them see the gift they have received and learn ways to respect and defend life. Amen.

The Value of Life

Snapshots

On any given day, if you surf through the headlines, you might see these snapshots of life:

- A two-year-old girl is killed by gunfire from a passing car as the result of gang members firing at one another. Gang members considered her collateral damage.
- Top scientists promote new reproductive technologies as a means to enhance your current lifestyle, paving the way for an age of eugenics. Eugenics is the science that seeks to eliminate "undesirable" hereditary qualities of a person or race.
- The current pop star reaches peak celebrity status yielding more headlines due to a risqué music video.
- A medical group proposes that health-care costs would be reduced if we helped the elderly to die.

Sadly, we live in a society too often enslaved by the consequences of Original Sin, by sin and evil. We witness a disregard for the sacredness of human life all around us. Underneath it all is a view that a person is merely a thing to be used instead of a person to love.

Look again. There are other snapshots. You might not see them often, but they are just as real:

- A religious order works with gang members to break their cycle of violence through job assistance and counseling.
- A production company hits mainstream with a new movie about the gifts of life and love.
- Teens go on an alternative spring break mission trip to work alongside the poor in Guatemala.
- Members of a parish peacefully protest outside an abortion facility, offering sidewalk counseling while praying for a change of heart.

This lesson will help you to:

- **explore** ways society values human life.
- **examine** some major threats to human life.
- **evaluate** attitudes that can change behavior to promote life.

What kind of snapshots from life have you noticed this week?

The Value of Life 35

Teaching Tip

Family Violence: Violence can erupt anywhere. In fact families can experience violence. Domestic violence is especially hurtful because it happens between people who are called to love each other as spouses, parents or siblings, etc. When violence happens in a family, outside help should be sought. One of the most tragic forms of family violence is when a family member commits suicide. It is important to pray for that person and others who were close. Students suffering from these experiences need to have trusted adults in whom they can confide.

Objective

To examine how society views the value of human life

Pray

Pray for an increase in respect for all life, especially for the unborn and all those suffering from injustice.

Focus

In small groups, have students develop a common definition of *violence* and then one for *sacred.* Have them also cite three examples for each.

Discover

- Divide students into six groups. Assign each group a period of four hours in a day, such as 4 am to 10 am. Have each group find one significant news item that occurred during their time.
- Direct them to write a headline that sums up their news item. Then gather them to discuss as a class if their headline reflects the violence in life or life as sacred.
- Read "Snapshots." Allow students to ask questions about the reading.

- Time permitting, discuss further examples of snapshots from life, locally at home, in their school, parish or community. As well, explore with students by identifying people they would feel comfortable talking with if they experienced violence.

TEACH

Objective

To identify some major threats to human life

Focus

- Survey students' attitudes toward "life issues." Using the six bolded terms in this section, ask if the students are interested in making a difference; sympathetic but nothing I can do; or apathetic, not my concern.
- Have students discuss reasons for their attitude.

Explore

- Have students quietly read "Look Again." As a class read it aloud, pause for students to react or ask questions.
- Ask students to identify other important life issues, including child abuse. Have them identify various forms of child abuse. Help them to understand that child abuse can be more than inappropriate touching. Remind them that child abuse is never the fault of the child.
- Place students in groups, with each group assigned one of the six threats to human life. Each group needs to have a leader to facilitate the discussion, a secretary to make a record of the group's discussion and a reporter who will present their summary.

Catholics Believe

Human life is sacred and the fundamental right to life comes from our God-given inherent dignity. The dignity of every person is rooted in the fact that every person has been created in the image and likeness of God.

Look Again

The differences in the snapshots of life that were presented on the previous page is respect. Part of maturing in God's love involves learning to see all human life with "eyes of respect." The English word *respect* comes from the Latin word *respectare*, which means "to look again." We need "to look again" at how we view human life.

As we deepen in our relationship with God, we grow in our desire to want what Jesus wants and to reject what Jesus rejects. Jesus and his followers consistently valued and worked to promote the dignity of every person, especially those most vulnerable.

Today, there remain many major threats to human life. Among these threats, which we are called to reject, are:

Pope John Paul II and Mehmet Ali Agca

- **Murder.** Murder is the direct and intentional killing of an innocent person. Murder is never justifiable no matter a person's circumstance, and is always a grave sin.
- **Direct or deliberate abortion.** Direct or deliberate abortion is the direct killing of the unborn human person growing inside the womb of the mother. Abortion is also a grave sin, and leaves serious trauma for those involved, especially the mother.
- **Euthanasia.** Euthanasia is the deliberate, unjust killing of a person who is elderly, severely disabled, or suffering from serious or terminal illness.

When we look again at each of these evil and gravely sinful acts, we see the need to reject them and to work to restore respect for the value of every person at every stage of life–from conception to natural death. In addition, we also need to look again at war and capital punishment, widespread acts which society and the Church do not always look at in the same way.

Think about the major threats to human life that you see today.

36 The Value of Life

Teaching Tip

Violent Abuse: Violence can take many forms. While physical aggression is perhaps most known, violence can also be verbal, emotional and psychological, and even spiritual. Teasing, bullying and sexual harassment are different forms of violence. Some of the most severe forms of abuse are sexual assault, sexual abuse and murder. Abuse causes severe problems for individuals and society. Abuse victims are more likely to experience homelessness, addiction and prostitution than people who have not been abused. People who abuse others were often victims of abuse themselves, thus perpetuating the cycle of abuse and violence. All violence and self-abusive behavior violate God's Law of Love and reject the Church's teachings, especially respect for human dignity.

The dignity of the human person is also threatened by other heinous acts that do not always directly end human life. We are always to reject these acts, which violate the dignity of the human person.

- **Terrorism.** Terrorism includes a variety of violent acts for the sole purpose of causing intense violent fear upon a person or group of people. Unjust acts of armed conflict, torture, and kidnapping all constitute forms of terrorism.
- **Misuse of reproductive technology.** Technology often perverts science by placing the capability of the scientist above the dignity of the person in ways that are contrary to God's Law and the teachings of the Church. Such misuses contradict the conjugal act of love and degrade people.
- **Poverty and discrimination.** Poverty and discrimination remain perhaps among the greatest global sources of violence. Because these acts often deprive people of the basic necessities of life, they violate the dignity of people.

The only way to break the cycle of violence that always threatens human life is to look again with the "eyes of respect" and show our love for every person as God does. Living every moment with respect for the dignity of the human person is what Jesus did and what we are to do. When we do, we help to create a *consistent ethic of life*. In other words, all that we do reflects the love of God.

Growing in Virtue

Violence in many forms threatens human life and violates the dignity of people. Learning to see and treat each other with **respect** develops a consistent ethic of life and can help break the cycle of violence. When we live a consistent ethic of life, we desire and want what God desires and wants for all people.

"Taking a Stand"

In a small group, choose one of the threats to life mentioned. Make a list of three practical things eighth-graders can do to stand up to this threat.

Terrorism.

Misuse of reproductive technology.

Poverty and discrimination.

Extending the Lesson

Using Activity Master 5A: Use the Activity Master "Reading About Violence." This activity helps students further research current events in the news that depict a violent event as well as one that shows respect for life. Then students are asked to reflect on each.

Global Awareness: Have students research how a major threat to life anywhere in the world can have a local impact. An example includes how a parish assists refugees from war-torn countries who seek asylum in the United States. Or how many youth groups take mission trips to poverty-stricken countries to help build or rebuild infrastructure to access needed food, safe water or general utilities.

TEACH

- Each group is to define clearly the threat, explain how each threat violates the dignity of the human person, and how society can work toward a healthy and holy view of the human person.
- Assign a small group child abuse as its issue. What can eighth graders do to prevent child abuse? Focus on speaking out against abuse and encouraging people who have been abused to tell someone what has happened to them.
- Before the groups begin, review the terms *respect* and *dignity* by reading the Catholics Believe and Growing in Virtue boxes.
- Be sure to monitor the groups as they work to clarify any questions that might arise.
- Have each group report to the class on what they discussed. Discuss how consistent the views were and the applications of respecting human life for all of the issues.

Connect

- Have students discuss their understanding of "consistent ethic of life." Be sure to point out that the right to life comes from God and every person from conception to natural death has that right.
- Have students remain in their groups to complete the activity on the page.
- Time permitting, have students debate whether we live in a "culture of death" or a "culture of life."

APPLY

Objective

To evaluate attitudes in order to promote change with action

Focus

Read, the Catholic Family Album box. Inquire: When you get to high school, what kind of life issues projects will you look for? What can you do today to prepare for them?

Discover

Read aloud Matthew 15:10–20. Inquire: How is it true that what comes from the heart and out of the mouth defiles a person? Explain that defiles means to corrupt the pure, to contaminate the good or desecrate the sacred.

Integrate

- Read the text on the page. Discuss how our attitudes come from our hearts.
- Respond to any questions students may have about the activity on the page. Have students complete the activity on the page in groups.
- Time permitting, have students research online the Catholic Campaign for Human Development and its youth section.

Pray

Pray for an increase in respect for all life, especially for the unborn and all those suffering from injustice.

Catholic Family Album

Cyber Bridges is a project of Catholic Relief Services connecting the Catholic youth in the United States with the marginalized youth in overseas programs. The overall goal of the project is to provide the necessary means for youth across the globe to build sustainable relationships based on solidarity and respect. Through school participation, each student participant is involved over three years building six bridges. Each bridge is a conversation based on a topic to facilitate collaborative learning and mutual respect.

Making Attitude Adjustments

Making a difference in the world begins with adjusting attitudes and changing hearts. We begin by naming and reflecting on our own attitudes and cooperating with the grace of the Holy Spirit to align our attitudes with those of Jesus. Adjusting attitudes is never easy and it usually takes a lifetime.

The chart below contains several attitudes that undermine living a consistent ethic of life. A person who has a consistent ethic of life always values and respects human life in making their decisions. Read and think about each and then suggest an "attitude adjustment" that might make a difference in the way a person values human life. Add any other attitudes that you know need adjusting. Share your chart with the class. Then in private take a personal assessment of your own attitudes toward life. Identify and name those that need adjusting. In your journal or notebook, write a prayer asking God for a change of heart.

ATTITUDE	ADJUSTMENT
"This pregnancy is an inconvenience."	
"Some people are just stupid."	
"Life with a serious disability has little value."	
"If somebody hurts you, hurt them back worse."	
"Life with suffering isn't worth living."	

38 The Value of Life

Extending the Lesson

Using Activity Master 5B: Use the Activity Master "Celebrating People." This activity helps students consider looking again at the positive influences and actions in society, especially those close to home.

Guest Speaker: Invite a guest speaker from the diocesan or parish pro-life committee to address any of the major threats to human life that the students have studied. Be sure the speaker is experienced in speaking with youth. An alternative is to invite the local parish youth minister to speak about what the parish's youth group does to promote and advocate on behalf of pro-life issues.

ONLINE ACTIVITIES FOR LESSON 5

Activity Master 5A

Name ....

Reading about Violence

Find one news story about a violent event, and one that shows respect for life. Share your answers with your classmates.

The Violent Story

1. What was the story about?
2. Was the story straightforward or sensationalized?
3. If there were photographs, what did they show?

The Respect-for-Life Story

1. What was the story about?
2. Could you tell how the reporter felt about the story? What words gave you clues about his or her feelings?
3. If there were photographs, what did they show?

Your Opinion

1. Why do you think some newspapers give more space to dramatic, violent stories than to respect-for-life stories?
2. What's wrong with showing violence in the media?

Activity Master 5B

Name ....

Celebrating People

Respect means "to look again." Practice taking a fresh look at yourself and at people close to you. You may find hidden treasures! Choose from the list of qualities below, or think of your own.

compassion	**kindness**
cheerfulness	**patience**
creativity	**sense of humor**
enthusiasm	**sense of justice**
honesty	**tolerance**
intelligence	**unselfishness**

Choose three qualities to celebrate in:

1. a family member
2. a close friend
3. a classmate
4. a famous person you admire
5. someone you find hard to like
6. yourself

How to Find It
How to Use It

Step 1: Click & Select

Go to RCLBFamilyLife.com
Click on the link for activities.
Then select the activity master you need.

Step 2: Print & Copy

Print each activity master in advance.
Then copy enough for everyone in the class.

Step 3: Share & Discuss

Once students have completed the activity, have them share and discuss their responses.

LESSON 6 PLANNER

Goal: To investigate behavior and actions that are or can be harmful or dangerous to a person's health and identify strategies for making healthy choices

Engage
Page 71

Objective
To explore the impact of choices to your health

Pray
Prayer of thanksgiving

Focus
Discuss tactics for teaching how to ride a bicycle.

Discover
Debate the effectiveness of scare tactics.

Teach
Page 72

Objective
To understand the risks and dangers of harmful substances

Focus
Catholics Believe: Scandal is contrary to respecting people.

Explore
Read, discuss and summarize the importance of learning about health in order to form good habits based upon informed decisions.

Connect
Growing in Virtue: Good judgment and respect
Create a list of healthy choices for eighth-grade students.

Apply
Page 74

Objective
To create strategies for making healthy choices

Focus
Catholic Family Album: Saint Maximilian Kolbe

Discover
List trusted or admirable adults.

Integrate
Create prescriptions for health: physical, emotional and spiritual.

Pray
Intercessory Prayer

Reviewing Unit 3
Summarize and review the content from both lessons.

Vocabulary Preview

Anorexia—an eating disorder of habitually fasting and rigorous exercise based on an obsessive fear of being fat

Bulimia—an eating disorder in which victims go through cycles of binging and purging

Nicotine—an addictive substance that is inhaled in cigarette smoke

Respect—to show honor for a person because they have been created in the image and likeness of God

Scandal—behavior that leads another to do evil

Materials Needed

- writing paper
- pens, pencils
- art supplies
- bottle of water
- Bible
- Lesson 6 Activity Masters

Call to Prayer

God our Father, you gave me the gift of life and the promise of eternal life. In gratitude for this gift and promise, I will try to care for myself physically and spiritually. Help my students be grateful for these same gifts. Amen.

Stay Healthy

Words to the Wise

"I don't care," David said, tossing his lunch in the trash can. "I still say they're just trying to scare us." His friends shook their heads as they discussed this morning's special assembly.

Two speakers had addressed the students. They were two bright people with frightening stories. The first speaker, Angela, was a thin, pretty young woman. She said, "My problems with eating started when I was in seventh grade. I'd see a model in a magazine and I'd go crazy. I thought I looked so fat! I tried everything to get thinner: not eating, throwing up, over-exercising. I almost killed myself. Luckily, my family and my doctor helped me. I got counseling and was in the hospital for three weeks. Now my anorexia is under control."

"In some ways, I'm lucky, too," said the other speaker, a guy named Jeff. He continued, "I started drinking when I was in junior high. I thought it made me seem funnier and smarter. Now I'm nineteen, and I've been sober for a year." Jeff swallowed and continued, "One thing I'll never forget is knowing that I killed someone. I was drunk the night of prom and went driving. I crashed the car, and my girlfriend was killed. Her parents tell me they've forgiven me, but I'm still working on forgiving myself."

Back at the lunch table, David looked at his friends scornfully, "C'mon guys," he said, "Don't you know this is a typical adult scam? They exaggerate the dangers of everything so we won't even try to have fun."

"I don't know," Robbie responded. "Hospitals, anorexia, drinking, car crashes, death. Doesn't sound like much fun to me."

This lesson will help you to:

- **explore** the impact of choices to your health.
- **understand** the risks and dangers of harmful substances.
- **create** strategies for making choices that promote your health and well being.

If you were part of this conversation, what would you say to the group?

Stay Healthy 39

Teaching Tip

Depression and Disorders: We used to think that depression was only an adult condition. But today we know that anyone at any age can be depressed. It is important to advise youth who experience depression or continued sadness to talk to someone about this. Encourage them to talk with their parents or other trusted adults. The same advice can be given concerning other harmful situations, such as eating disorders or the use of harmful substances.

Child Safety: You may wish to address the following facts about sexual grooming as you review the content from Lesson 6 about healthy choices.

Sex offenders often groom their victims for weeks, months, and even years before they initiate sexual contact. During the grooming phase, offenders often lead their victims to believe that they are willing participants in the process, and therefore, that the abuse is somehow their fault.

ENGAGE

Objective

To explore the impact of choices to your health

Pray

Open the lesson with a prayer thanking God for the gift of health.

Focus

Have students discuss what tactics they might use to help a child learn how to safely ride a bicycle. Tactics might include modeling, scaring, threatening, rewarding, etc.

Discover

- Read "Words to the Wise." Allow students to ask questions about the reading.
- Divide the class into two groups to debate the effectiveness of scare tactics. One groups is to argue from the point of David, while the other group argues from the point of Robbie.
- Inquire: What tactic or method do you think would best deter students your age from choosing harmful and unhealthy habits? Why?
- Time permitting, have students privately write about a personal goal in choosing to live a healthy and holy life, starting today.

TEACH

Objective

To understand the risks and dangers of harmful substances

Focus

- Inquire: How would you define "scandal"? What are some examples of it?
- Read the Catholics Believe box. Explain that scandals often involve misleading or false information. Others who know better lure their victims into doing something known to be wrong or sinful.

Explore

- As a class read the text aloud; pause for students to react or ask questions.
- Explain that knowing the facts about harmful substances can help a person avoid scandal by rejecting the sin therein.
- Invite a volunteer to drink from an unmarked and unused bottle of water. Have the volunteer "think out loud" about the offer. Observe their response. Do not give the student the water.
- Go through the same scenario step by step to discern whether or not the bottle of water is safe. Use the following: (1) Can I trust this person? (2) Do I know with certainty that this is safe? (3) What potential harm is there in using it? (4) Am I okay without it? (5) What real good would it do me in using it? (6) Would I offer it to someone whom I care about?

Catholics Believe

Scandal is behavior which leads another to do evil. Respect for the person demands that the gifts of life and health be seen as precious. Certain drugs inflict grave harm on the person. Cooperation in their use by selling drugs is not only illegal but is morally wrong and sinful. It is a cause of scandal and contributes to the harm of another person.

A Firm Foundation

Learning as much as you can about what is good for you and what is not helps you make intelligent decisions.

A Balanced Diet

Food is important for everyone. Eating a variety of healthful foods in amounts according to your body's needs maintains your health. You have learned by now that eating too little or too much has harmful effects on our bodies. However, did you know that the kinds and amounts of food also affect how you feel? Like so many things in life, what makes a good diet is balance.

Tobacco and Alcohol

The health problems associated with smoking, such as lung cancer, heart disease, breathing problems, and mouth cancer are well known. But some people smoke and chew tobacco anyway. Nicotine, the key ingredient in tobacco, is addictive. The tars and gases released in cigarette smoke are also highly toxic. The best health habit you can develop with regard to tobacco is to leave it alone. Don't smoke or use tobacco and don't hang around with people who do.

Used properly by adults, wines and liquors can add enjoyment to a meal or social occasion. But used improperly, these same beverages can lead to suffering and death. Some people have a tendency to become addicted to alcohol and therefore should not drink it at all. Pregnant women should avoid alcohol because it may cause problems for the baby. People who are driving or operating machinery should not drink because even a small amount of alcohol affects concentration, slows the reflexes, and impairs one's ability to function responsibly.

Think about what you know regarding harmful and dangerous substances.

Drinking alcohol has dangers for young people especially. Alcohol has a harmful effect on growing bodies. It also removes inhibitions, making people more likely to indulge in reckless behavior or sexual activity. The best health decision you can make now is to postpone using alcohol until you're an adult, and then to use it only with moderation.

40 Stay Healthy

Teaching Tip

Good Decisions: Good decisions require careful thought. People who make good decisions generally follow a few simple rules. (1) They focus only on what is most important. (2) They might break larger decisions into smaller ones. (3) They choose what is right and good, avoiding what would violate their own integrity. (4) They consider the positive results that might come from their decision, as well as the negative. (5) They determine how they will implement their decision because decisions without plans rarely get implemented. (6) They try to keep things simple. (7) They consider as many options as possible. Making good decisions usually leads people to make more good decisions. Conversely, poor choices often lead to additional poor choices down the road.

Drugs

If someone walked up to you and asked you to swallow poison, you'd be smart enough to say no. But every day thousands of otherwise intelligent young people put poison into their bodies by abusing drugs. Don't let anybody fool you; there is no such thing as a little poison. Certain drugs are illegal because of the severe risk of injury or death. Again, the best thing to do with drugs is to stay clear. You won't miss anything by avoiding drugs. But by getting involved with drugs, you could miss the rest of your life. If you've started using drugs or you know someone who has, get help now.

Growing in Virtue

Good judgment in making choices about your physical, emotional, and spiritual health shows respect for yourself, others, and God. Making good judgments about caring for your physical and spiritual health can often be the first step in a major lifestyle change that can result in a healthier emotional and spiritual life.

"Health Checklist"

Make a list of good health choices eighth-graders can make. Compile a collection of lists to make a booklet to share with other teens.

Extending the Lesson

Using Activity Master 6A: Use the Activity Master "The Effects of Alcohol and Tobacco." This activity helps students to further learn about the negative effects of alcohol and tobacco on the human body.

Friendly Advice: Have students write a fictitious teen newspaper column in which a teen reader asks the columnist how to break a personal unhealthy habit. The bad or unhealthy habits could be drugs, smoking, non-marital sex, drinking, eating disorder, etc. Invite volunteers to share with the class their column. As a class discuss the advice the students offer in their column.

- When discussing the concepts of free will, choice, and sin, remind students that abuse is never their fault. Tell the students that people who abuse drugs, alcohol and food often have low self-esteem and lack self-respect.
- Discuss this question: "Why do some teens have poor self-respect?" Have the students identify ways that teens can improve their self-esteem.

- Remind students that God loves them and that they can never lose that love no matter what choices they make or what happens to them.

Connect

- Have students read the Growing in Virtue box. Explain how making good decisions about our physical health can positively affect our spiritual health. For example, if I am overly tired, I may choose not to pray or go to Mass.
- Have students complete the activity on the page. Then as a class, compile a top ten list of healthy choices that they will commit to maintaining the rest of the week.
- Time permitting, have students list what they believe to be effective tactics for promoting healthy choices at their age.

APPLY

Objective

To create strategies for making healthy choices

Focus

Read the Catholic Family Album box. Ask: How was Saint Maximilian a model of spiritual health, despite his physical illness? *(He had become so spiritually strong that he offered himself to save the life of another at Auschwitz.)*

Discover

- Have students list the names of trusted or admirable adults from whom they would seek advice. Elicit from them their reasons, ensuring reliability in the overall list.
- Be sure the list represents all aspects of healthy and holy living: intellectual, physical, emotional and spiritual.

Integrate

- Read "To Your Health." Respond to any questions students may have about the activity on the page.
- Have students complete the activity on the page.

Pray

Pray for the intercession of Saint Maximilian Kolbe in respecting life through healthy choices.

Catholic Family Album

Saint Maximilian Kolbe suffered poor health during his life. Despite these sufferings, he lived his life out of love for God and others. Suffering from tuberculosis and nearly dying, Maximilian continued to focus on living his faith even while suffering with the illness. He eventually traveled to Japan and India, where he worked as a missionary. Poor health forced him to return home, where he was eventually arrested and sent to the concentration camp at Auschwitz. There he sacrificed his life for others. Throughout his life, Maximilian was a man of great spiritual health despite his poor physical health.

To Your Health

Caring for your physical health is an important aspect of showing respect for God's gift of life. You can make good health choices in other areas too:

- You can care for your emotional health. Caring for your emotional health means being patient with yourself as you go through the changes and stresses of puberty.
- You can care for your spiritual health. Caring for your spiritual health or well-being means spending time reading Scripture, going to Mass, praying quietly before the Blessed Sacrament, living the Corporal and Spiritual Works of Mercy, and putting your faith into action in other ways.

Making the right choices for your physical, emotional, and spiritual health is caring for your whole self, body and soul. On each of the prescription forms below, write one good habit you can begin or continue practicing this week. Then monitor your progress into the future.

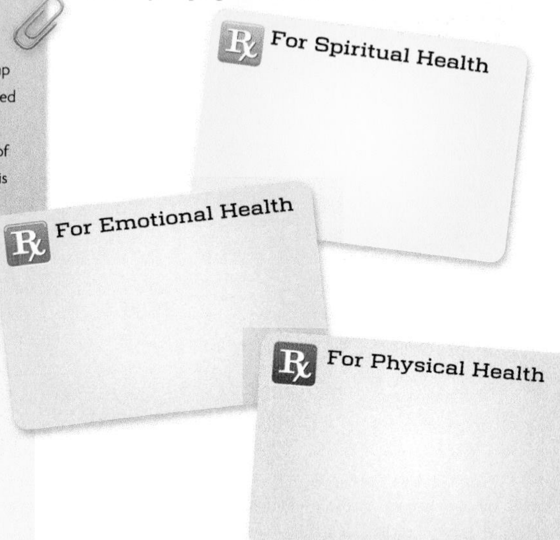

42 Stay Healthy

Extending the Lesson

Using Activity Master 6B: Use the Activity Master "Reasons and Responses." This activity helps students to further develop communication skills on how to best respond to misguided attitudes and misinformed reasons for choosing bad or unhealthy habits.

Prescriptions for Health: Invite students to submit their prescription forms from the activity on slips of paper. Review them for appropriateness and then post them for public reading. Explain that this collection of suggestions for healthy living can be a daily reminder on how to form a habit of choosing what is good, healthy and holy.

ONLINE ACTIVITIES FOR LESSON 6

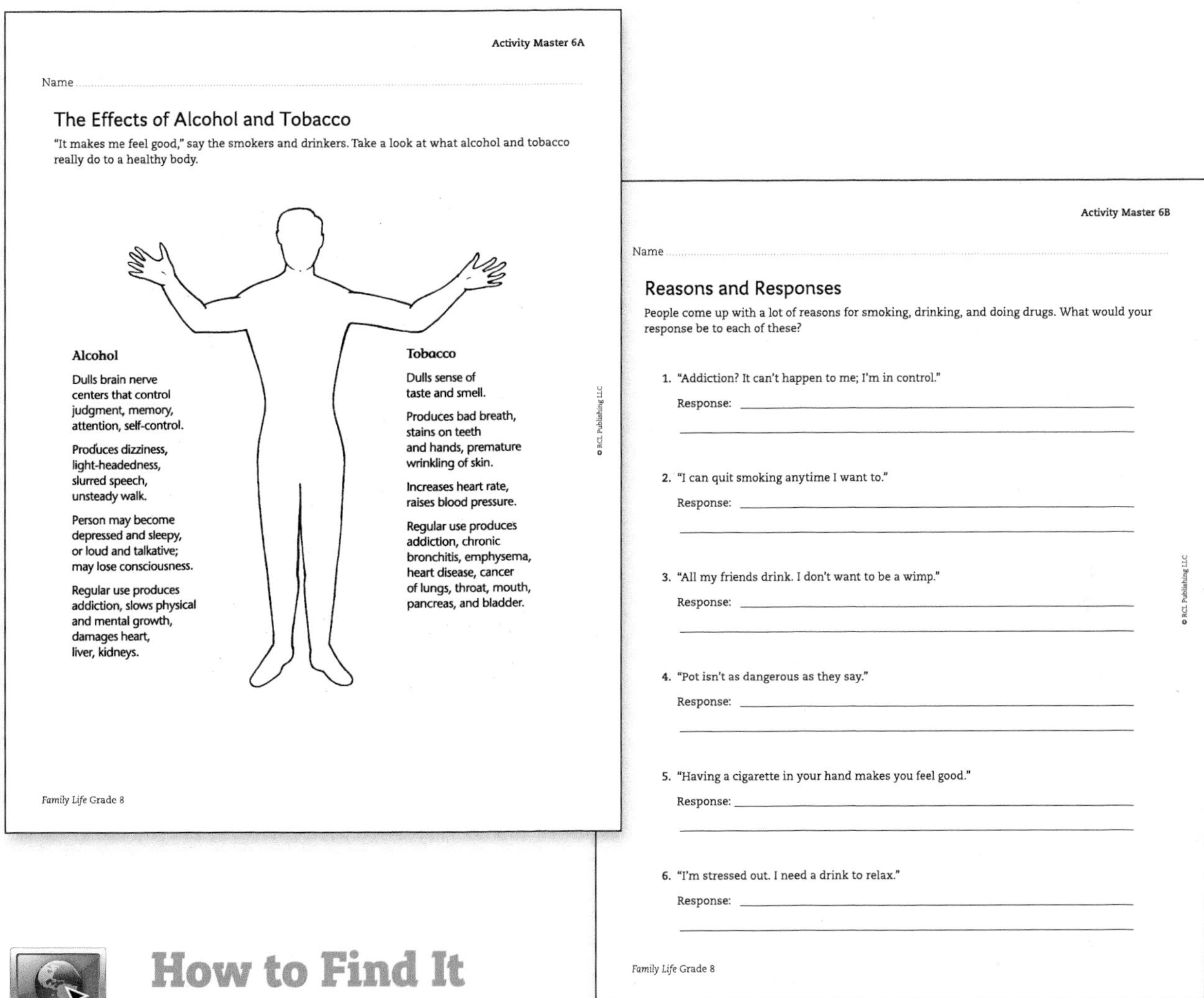

Activity Master 6A

Name

The Effects of Alcohol and Tobacco

"It makes me feel good," say the smokers and drinkers. Take a look at what alcohol and tobacco really do to a healthy body.

Alcohol

Dulls brain nerve centers that control judgment, memory, attention, self-control.

Produces dizziness, light-headedness, slurred speech, unsteady walk.

Person may become depressed and sleepy, or loud and talkative; may lose consciousness.

Regular use produces addiction, slows physical and mental growth, damages heart, liver, kidneys.

Tobacco

Dulls sense of taste and smell.

Produces bad breath, stains on teeth and hands, premature wrinkling of skin.

Increases heart rate, raises blood pressure.

Regular use produces addiction, chronic bronchitis, emphysema, heart disease, cancer of lungs, throat, mouth, pancreas, and bladder.

© RCL Publishing LLC

Family Life Grade 8

Activity Master 6B

Name

Reasons and Responses

People come up with a lot of reasons for smoking, drinking, and doing drugs. What would your response be to each of these?

1. "Addiction? It can't happen to me; I'm in control."
   Response:
2. "I can quit smoking anytime I want to."
   Response:
3. "All my friends drink. I don't want to be a wimp."
   Response:
4. "Pot isn't as dangerous as they say."
   Response:
5. "Having a cigarette in your hand makes you feel good."
   Response:
6. "I'm stressed out. I need a drink to relax."
   Response:

© RCL Publishing LLC

Family Life Grade 8

How to Find It
How to Use It

Step 1: Click & Select

Go to RCLBFamilyLife.com
Click on the link for activities.
Then select the activity master you need.

Step 2: Print & Copy

Print each activity master in advance.
Then copy enough for everyone in the class.

Step 3: Share & Discuss

Once students have completed the activity,
have them share and discuss their responses.

Summary

- Ask the students to read through the Summary section.
- Invite them to ask questions about any points that are not clear to them.
- Make sure to expand on any points that were perhaps touched on only lightly during class time.

Thinking It Through

- Have students answer all three questions on the page.
- Assign each student a number from one through three.
- Have students share with the class their answer to the question that corresponds to their assigned number.

Matching It Up

Use this matching section to help the students identify the appropriate definition or description of a key concept, term or person from the unit.

REVIEWING UNIT 3

Name ....

Summary

Remember what you have learned in each of the lessons in God's Gift of Life.

LESSON 5: The Value of Life

- Human life is a sacred gift from God. Each person has a fundamental dignity because everyone has been created in the image and likeness of God.
- Treating each other with respect can help break the cycle of violence in society.
- Sin and moral evil are at the root of the many threats against human life.

LESSON 6: Stay Healthy

- Showing respect for the dignity of the human person deters and prevents scandal.
- Abusive use of certain substances causes harm to a person, especially during adolescence.
- Making good choices about your physical, emotional, and spiritual health shows respect for the gift of your life.

Thinking It Through

1. What are the greatest threats to God's gift of life and how can they be overcome?
2. How does valuing and showing respect for the dignity of every person affect medical and health-care decisions?
3. How would you communicate to other teenagers the dangers of substance abuse?

Matching It Up

On each line, write the letter of the description in Column B that best goes with the term in Column A.

A

1. ....E.... Abortion
2. ....A.... Anorexia
3. ....B.... Murder
4. ....C.... Nicotine
5. ....D.... Scandal

B

A. Eating disorder of habitually fasting and rigorous exercise
B. The direct intentional killing of an innocent person
C. Addictive substance that is inhaled in cigarette smoke
D. Behavior that leads another to sin
E. The direct killing of the unborn human person growing inside the womb of the mother

Unit 3 Review 43

Teaching Tip

Child Safety: You may wish to address the following facts about sexual grooming as you review the content from Lesson 6 about healthy choices.

Sex offenders often groom their victims for weeks, months, and even years before they initiate sexual contact. During the grooming phase, offenders often lead their victims to believe that they are willing participants in the process, and therefore, that the abuse is somehow their fault.

REVIEWING UNIT 3

Name..

Recalling Key Concepts

Circle the T if the statement is true. Circle the F if the statement is false.

1. The word *respect* comes from the Latin *respectare*, meaning "to look again." (T) F
2. Often people make bad health choices because they have too much self-respect. T (F)
3. Major threats to human life include only those that end human life. T (F)
4. Learning about what is healthy can help a person make good decisions. (T) F
5. Bad health choices have little or no consequences. T (F)

Fill in the missing words in these sentences.

6. When reproductive technologies contradict the conjugal act of love and seek to eliminate certain "undesirable" genetic attributes of the human embryo, science promotes **EUGENICS**.
7. The key ingredient in tobacco, **NICOTINE**, is addictive.
8. When people do not have access to adequate food and water, local communities have a moral obligation to overcome these forms of **POVERTY**.
9. Having a diet with a variety of healthful foods in amounts according to your body's needs maintains your **HEALTH**.
10. Living always with respect for the dignity of the human person creates a **CONSISTENT ETHIC OF LIFE**.

Working Together

Some of the legal and illegal substances people abuse include beer, prescription drugs, marijuana, cocaine, cigarettes, and methamphetamines. In small groups, choose one of those substances. As a group, research the effects of its use on a person's health. Present your findings to the class.

44 Unit 3 Review

Teaching Tip

Substance Abuse: Take this opportunity to help students who may be aware of substance abuse among family members and/or friends. These students may be guarded or tend to protect individuals who are abusing. Honor their loyalty to their loved ones, but make available sources of help. Always check with school or parish policies regarding referrals. Meet with the proper authorities as required and share students' concerns about substance abuse among their peers. Search for effective and appropriate ways the students can address the problems.

Recalling Key Concepts

- Use this section to help the students be able to accurately recall the key concepts from the unit.
- For the true and false section, you can have students correct any false statements.
- To help with the fill-in-the-blank section, you might want to provide a word bank on the board.

Working Together

- Choose a project that best fits the needs and abilities of your students, as well as your time schedule.
- Time permitting, have students complete the unit assessment individually or as a class; otherwise, encourage them to complete it at home.

UNIT 4

God's Gift of Love

Background

*"Holy Mary, Mother of God, / you have given the world its true light, / Jesus, your Son—the Son of God. / You abandoned yourself completely / to God's call / and thus became a wellspring / of the goodness which flows from him. / Show us Jesus. Lead us to him. / Teach us to know and love him, / so that we too can become / capable of true love / and be fountains of living water / in the midst of a thirsting world" (*Deus Caritas Est *42).*

MARRIED LOVE IS A LIVING SIGN OF GOD'S FAITHFUL and life-giving love for humanity. Through the Sacrament of Matrimony a Christian marriage becomes a living sign of Christ's life-giving, faithful love for his Church. When Christian husbands and wives nurture and cherish each other, they become a living sacrament. They become a living sign of Christ's love at work in the world. The married couple become a community in which the Christian family learns to love and serve one another as Christ commanded, "As I have loved you, so you also should love one another" (John 13:34).

"The vocation to marriage is written in the very nature of man and woman as they came from the hand of the Creator" (*Catechism of the Catholic Church* 1603). A man and a woman marry because they desire and freely choose to share the totality of their life and love with each other forever. The quality "forever" gives witness to the reality of God's love for people. "Forever" also identifies that true self-giving, as God loves us and Christ loves his Church, never ends.

Additional Background

Catechism of the Catholic Church: §§ 1642, 1654, 1660, 1664, 2348–2350, 2365, 2368

The Church places before her members the vocation of lifelong, loving, faithful and indissoluble marriage. Young people need the living witnesses of parents and spouses who "strive to give *example and witness* with their own lives to fidelity to God and one another in the marriage covenant" (*Truth and Meaning of Human Sexuality* 102).

Marriage is challenging, difficult at times. Young people need to learn the meaning of fidelity "in good times and bad." The youth may have a negative view of marriage. They may have experienced a broken marriage of their parents. Yet the indissolubility of marriage remains. Holding up the ideal of marriage flows directly from God's desire that we live the life that Jesus called for, a life of deep and abiding love.

MARRIAGE IS A LIFE OF FAITHFUL LOVE. DISCERNING the call to be married is one of life's most serious responsibilities. While many young people may look forward to marriage and will marry, others may accept God's call to a life in the single state or in the celibate priesthood or vowed religious life.

As the young people move toward considering marriage, they are to be helped in understanding not only the nature of marriage, but also how to gain a better understanding of the persons they might marry. Marriage preparation or catechesis begins in the family, progresses though many types of formal and informal education. Once married, spouses will continue to grow in their appreciation and understanding of the sacred state of marriage.

For Reflection

Read and reflect on the following:

"[Parents'] example is especially decisive in adolescence, the phase when young people are looking for lived and attractive behavior models" *(*Truth and Meaning of Human Sexuality *102).*

- How faithful am I in keeping my commitments to my family?
- What might I guide the young people to discover that fidelity in friendships is one sign of a healthy friendship?

Child Safety

This unit helps students examine what it means to be in a healthy relationship and to recognize the warning signs for unhealthy relationships. The child safety messages students have learned can protect them from abuse, and will also help them to develop healthy relationships as they grow older and begin to date. Remind students that they have the right to be treated with dignity and respect; to say no if someone touches them inappropriately or asks them to do something that causes them embarrassment; to assert themselves and their values, and to pay attention to their instincts.

Family Focus

Life is always a mix of ideals and reality. The Church places before its members the vocation of lifelong, loving marriage. Everyone deserves to know about God's plan for marriage. Ideals don't disappear when we don't quite measure up. We are all called to do the best we can and if we fail, God is generous in his forgiveness. Invite parents to review materials in the Family Time pages and in the Parent Connection to discuss the gift of love.

LESSON 7 PLANNER

Goal: To learn ways to develop and deepen friendships using guidelines for healthy friendships through an understanding of Christian love

Engage

Page 81

Objective

To examine how to best build lasting relationships

Family Time

Ensure that each student tears out their Family Time page to complete at home.

Pray

Prayer for friendship

Focus

List top ten qualities of a good friend.

Discover

Discuss the role of parents in their child's relationships.

Teach

Page 82

Objective

To explore guidelines for nurturing healthy friendships

Focus

Assess the qualities of a good friend.

Explore

Read, discuss and summarize the importance of developing good friendships that can last a lifetime or prepare one for marriage.

Catholics Believe: The human capacity to love and procreate

Connect

Growing in Virtue: Modesty

Commit to a personal contract on developing healthy friendships.

Apply

Page 84

Objective

To encourage living a life based on Christian love

Focus

Catholic Family Album: Saint John of the Cross

Discover

I Corinthians 13:1–13

Integrate

Demonstrate authentic love.

Pray

Prayer to Saint John of the Cross

Vocabulary Preview

Divorce—a legal procedure declaring the end of a civil marriage; different from an annulment in the Catholic Church

Marriage—a covenantal relationship between a man and a woman in which their spousal love is to be unitive and procreative

Modesty—the practice of valuing and guarding the sacredness of the body through proper speech, attire and conduct

Sexuality—human capacity to love and form relationships based on being male or female

Materials Needed

- writing paper
- pens, pencils
- art supplies
- Bible
- Lesson 7 Activity Masters

Call to Prayer

O Holy Trinity, you are the divine community of love. Every gift of love I receive and give starts with your love for me. Help my students to love generously and responsibly. Guide them in finding healthy friendships. Amen.

Loving Together

The Dating Game

"By the way, mom, I'm going out with Megan," Sean announced from the backseat of the car, on the way to soccer practice.

His mother almost slammed on the brakes. "You're what?" she exclaimed. Then she said, "You are only in the eighth grade. You cannot drive yet. How can you be dating any girl, let alone go steady with Megan?"

Sean just rolled his eyes and let his little brother explain, "Mom, they don't date. Going out just means they're best friends. Ya know, always on the phone together."

This lesson will help you to:

- **explore** how to build lasting relationships.
- **learn** more about guidelines for having healthy friendships.
- **reflect** on and make choices to live a life based on the qualities of Christian love.

Building Relationships

Over the years the specific ways that people build friendships and relationships before marriage have somewhat changed. Sometimes this is called dating. Dating in its simplest form, as in Sean's and Megan's case, is companionship with a person of the other gender. It is spending time together and having fun together.

Not so long ago dating barely existed. Marriages were arranged, as they still are in some cultures today. From the 19th to early 20th centuries, building relationships for marriage was called courting. An unmarried couple would "call on" each other and have conversations in the family living room, often with parents within earshot.

For Sean and Megan, dating is a way of being close friends. Sean naturally told his mom about his relationship with Megan. In our society today, people do not marry as early as they did in the past. The teenage years for most young people is a time for building friendships. Later, during young adulthood, young men and young women focus specifically on building relationships that may lead to marriage. Now is a good time to build healthy friendships.

What are the advantages and disadvantages in having parents involved in your relationships?

Teaching Tip

Friendships Change Over Time: Over one's lifetime, the experience of friendship can change. During early years of childhood, a friend is simply someone to play with. Later on, friends take on other roles. They help young people feel accepted and have a sense of belonging. A friend can simply be someone to talk to or someone to be with. As a person grows and matures, their relationships, including friendships, do the same. At some point in life, a person realizes that they can have a friend for a reason, a friend for a season or a friend for a lifetime.

ENGAGE

Objective

To examine how to best build lasting relationships

Pray

Open the lesson with a prayer thanking God for friendship.

Focus

Have each student write a list of the top ten qualities of a good friend. Inquire: Would your parents approve this list? Would your best friend? As a class compile the top five qualities.

Discover

- In advance prepare three students to dramatize the "The Dating Game" section.
- Have students dramatize the opening story. Then read the remaining text "Building Relationships."
- Inquire: How realistic is the opening dialogue? Would one of your parents react in the same or in a similar fashion? Why?
- Ask: What role do parents have in their children's friendships? Explain that love moves us to care for one another. Friends watch over friends; parents watch over their children.
- Time permitting, have students dramatize a dialogue when Megan meets Sean's mom for the first time.

TEACH

Objective

To explore guidelines for nurturing healthy friendships

Focus

- Using the list of qualities of a good friend, pair-up students, boy and girl. They are to take on the opposite of their partner's list. For example, if the girl has clean-cut friend, the boy should act sloppy.
- As a class, sponsor a charades modeling event of three female volunteers and three male volunteers to walk the runway as "what not to be." Be clear that this is not a fashion show, but is about attitude and action.
- Review the reactions of the students. Though humorous at times, in real situations, they can go from irritating to disrespectful quickly.

Explore

- Have students quietly read "Relationship Rules." Read the Catholics Believe box. Inquire: What do you think about dating today as a way to practice divorce instead of marriage? What are some ways to avoid the practice of breaking-up a friendship?

- Organize the class into groups by gender, boys in one group, girls in another. Have each group make a list of what they want from a friendship with a member of the other gender and how they expect to be treated in that friendship.

Catholics Believe

Human sexuality affects all aspects of the human person, not just the body. Our sexuality is related to our capacity to love and to take part in God's plan for the creation of new life. Regarding all relationships, it is part of our natural ability to form appropriate relationships with others (see CCC 2332).

Relationship Rules

Even though eighth grade is too early to begin seriously thinking about marriage, it is a good time to build healthy friendships. In this way you can better prepare for marriage. Learning what it means to be a good friend before you commit to being a spouse is a healthy and natural thing to do.

Whether it is called "going steady," courting or dating, most exclusive relationships during adolescence are likely to break up. They rarely last until the boy and girl are mature enough to marry. These exclusive relationships often become training ground over time for breaking up a relationship. In other words, many of today's dating practices prepare you for divorce, not marriage. Relating to others as a faithful and trustworthy friend, especially in groups, is preferable to "pairing off" at this time in your life.

Think about what you learn about yourself and others when you are together in a group.

Enjoying each other's company by spending time together in groups is a healthy and fun way to develop friendships. By setting parameters in advance on how to develop healthy friendships, you can better focus on just being yourself, which includes maturing in self-knowledge. Here are some ways you can develop friendships with respect and honesty:

- **Respect others and yourself.** Respect the people you are with. Respect their feelings, needs, and values. Respect your family's and your friends' family rules. For example, follow curfews set up by your family and your friends' families.
- **Make arrangements.** Anyone can initiate a gathering of friends. If you are taking the lead, be specific about the plan and allow some flexibility so others can contribute. Share your plans with your family. Be sure family members know where you're going in case they need to reach you in an emergency.

48 Loving Together

Teaching Tip

Nine Steps for Developing a Healthy Relationship

1. Talk openly with your friend about beliefs and values.
2. Make decisions based on what you know is right and not on what everybody else is doing.
3. Treat others as equals, with dignity and respect.
4. Say good things about others and don't allow the criticisms of others to bring you down.
5. Be assertive with your answers; leave no doubts about what you want or do not want.
6. Allow relationships to develop naturally; don't predetermine how a relationship should be.
7. Have many close friends; do not partner-up quickly.
8. Believe in your right to set limits and make decisions for yourself.
9. Trust in yourself to do what is right and good.

- **Be courteous.** Do not force others to join or be upset if others do not join. When you are being invited, be gracious and honest in your response. Throughout the entire time, let your words and actions always express respect.
- **Look your best.** Neatness, cleanliness, and good grooming are signs of respect for yourself and others. Modesty and comfort are key.
- **Be responsible.** If you commit to being somewhere, be there, or communicate if you cannot. Changing plans at the last minute can be a sign of disrespect. Following plans and good rules is a sign of respect for all involved.

These guidelines for developing and deepening healthy friendships will help you to grow in self-knowledge and knowledge of others. They will help you learn how to participate in healthy and safe relationships. The attitude and the actions of self-respect or modesty are the foundation for developing friendships that could last a lifetime.

Growing in Virtue

Modesty is a virtue that protects the mystery of the person. Self-knowledge and self-preservation are two key aspects of modesty, or self-respect, that are necessary for healthy friendships. Being able to learn more about ourselves as God created us to be is a skill gained in forming relationships.

"Contract for Friendship"

Write your own contract committing yourself to developing and deepening friendships according to good rules that you will follow. Share with your family.

- Discuss the lists as a class. How are they similar? Different? Compile an appropriate class list and post it on the board. Remind students that they should insist that they be treated with dignity and respect by everyone in every relationship.

Connect

- Have students read the Growing in Virtue box. Explain: The guidelines are ways in which a person can enhance self-preservation through modesty; that is, looking your best reflects the best of who you are.
- Explain that because it can be difficult to see our real self, we need others to help us. Each of us also needs to make a commitment to ourselves to show the good person we are.
- Have students complete the activity on the page. Explain that the commitment we give to others in friendship can help us keep future commitments we make for ourselves.
- Have students discuss the benefits of hanging out in groups of friends more so than just with one other person in pairs.

Extending the Lesson

Using Activity Master 7A: Use the Activity Master "Dating Customs." This activity helps students to explore the dating customs from the past and compare them to those today.

Cartoon Strip: Direct students to create a three- to five-frame cartoon strip for a series related to friendship. The title of the series is "What's Wrong With This Picture?" Have students include speech balloons within the illustration. They may want to have a popular newspaper or web site cartoon strip available to model from. To help facilitate this activity, pair up students so they can collaborate on the development, writing and illustration of the cartoon strip.

APPLY

Objective

To encourage living a life based on Christian love

Focus

Read the Catholic Family Album box. Inquire: What do you think about Saint John of the Cross' imagery of love being like a living flame in the soul of a person? How does this symbol connect with qualities of love?

Discover

- Have students read I Corinthians 13:1–13. Inquire: How is an unloving person like a clashing cymbal?
- Be sure to clarify the meaning of any words that the students are not familiar with or do not know.

Integrate

- Read "Recognizing Christian Love." Respond to any questions students may have about the activity on the page.
- Have students complete the activity on the page. Then share as a class examples of each.

Pray

Pray for the intercession of Saint John of the Cross in seeking to understand and live with deep Christian love.

Catholic Family Album

Saint John of the Cross (1542–1591) wrote once that love is like a taste of eternal life, a touch of God, or a living flame in the soul of a person. Both he and Saint Teresa of Ávila (Teresa of Jesus, 1515–1582), a fellow Discalced Carmelite, had a profound friendship centered on Christ. They shared a similar vision on how to live for Christ and supported each other in developing the Discalced Carmelite religious order. Today both Saints are recognized as Doctors of the Church.

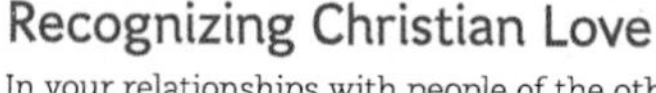

Recognizing Christian Love

In your relationships with people of the other gender, it is very important to learn to recognize aspects of authentic Christian love when you experience it. Saint Paul's description is a good starting point. Read what Saint Paul has to say about love. Read 1 Corinthians 13.

For each description below, write an example of how you might demonstrate that quality of authentic Christian love.

1. Love is patient.
2. Love is kind.
3. Love is not pompous.
4. Love is not rude.
5. Love is not quick-tempered.
6. Love rejoices with the truth.
7. Love believes all things.
8. Love hopes for all things.
9. Love endures all things.
10. Love never fails.

50 Loving Together

Extending the Lesson

Using Activity Master 7B: Use the Activity Master "Social Skills." This activity helps students to compare and apply the family happiness skills to other relationships like dating or friendships.

Language of Love: Write on the board "love" in the following languages: "amore" (Italian), "amour" (French), "amor" (Spanish), "liebe" (German), "sarang" (Korean), "ai" (Japanese), "aire" (Chinese), "eros" (Greek), "yeu" (Vietnamese). Have any students who can speak any of these languages (or others not listed) to read the word and use it in a complete sentence, translating what they said.

Activity Master 7A

Name ....

Dating Customs

Read what people from two past generations say about dating during their teens. Then, project yourself into the future. Explain the dating customs of your time to a teenager.

1910–1920

"When I was in my teens, 'dating' consisted of walking home from school or choir practice together, or maybe walking in the country with a group of friends. It was very casual; we just enjoyed each other as friends. There was no social pressure to have sex or make premature commitments. Eventually, you paired off, and then courtship began."

1940–1950

"People had just begun to take notice of the fads and lifestyle of 'teens.' So I think we were rather self-conscious about dating. Girls developed sort of a 'dating personality'—very bubbly, bouncy, and artificial. Boys usually decided where to go and paid for tickets, food, and such. Music and movies talked about 'being in love,' but not about 'making love.' "

Now

Explain the teen dating customs of your time and community to a teenager of the future.

Family Life Grade 8

Activity Master 7B

Name ....

Social Skills

Take a second look at the family happiness skills you read about in lesson one and the rules in lesson seven, and apply them here.

1. Respect: consideration for others' needs, feelings, and gifts

   You and your friends are into skating, but your date isn't. At the skating center, he or she is trying hard, but is looking very awkward and interfering with your fun. What are you going to do and say?

2. Affirmation: the skill of acknowledging the importance of someone

   You're out with a group of friends. There's a person of the other sex with you who is new to the group, and acting a little shy. What can you do?

3. Generosity: being humble and willing to give for the sake of another

   Your date is always fun to be with. But on this occasion, he or she seems very quiet and withdrawn. How will you handle this?

4. Communication: the skill of two-way conversation

   At a friend's party, you're sitting next to a classmate you don't know very well. What two questions could you ask to get a conversation started?

Family Life Grade 8

How to Find It
How to Use It

Step 1: Click & Select

Go to RCLBFamilyLife.com
Click on the link for activities.
Then select the activity master you need.

Step 2: Print & Copy

Print each activity master in advance.
Then copy enough for everyone in the class.

Step 3: Share & Discuss

Once students have completed the activity, have them share and discuss their responses.

LESSON 8 PLANNER

Goal: To explore God's plan for marriage and family by understanding the two purposes of marriage and learn ways to raise a healthy and holy family

Engage

Page 87

Objective

To recognize that marriage is but one vocation

Pray

Prayer for marriage and family

Focus

Share experiences of a wedding.

Discover

Discuss how major life events are ritualized.

Teach

Page 88

Objective

To understand the two purposes of marriage

Focus

Mark 10:1–12

Explore

Read, discuss and summarize the importance of commitment and fidelity in understanding the two purposes of marriage as planned by God.

Catholics Believe: Sacramental grace in marriage

Growing in Virtue: Fidelity

Connect

Thank parents for their commitment in love to the family.

Apply

Page 90

Objective

To explore how the Fruits of the Holy Spirit guide family life

Focus

Catholic Family Album: Blessed Zélie Martin

Discover

Galatians 5:13–26

Integrate

Record examples in life of the Fruits of the Holy Spirit.

Pray

Intercessory prayer

Reviewing Unit 4

Summarize and review the content from both lessons.

Vocabulary Preview

Conjugal Act of Love—sexual intercourse between husband and wife as an expression of their free, faithful, full and forever loving commitment as spouses

Contraception—the mentality and practice of separating the conjugal act from its two purposes of self-giving and life-giving

Premarital Sex—all sexual activity before marriage, violating the dignity of marriage

Vocation—the gift of God's calling to a particular way of life: single, married, ordained or consecrated; and our response to holiness in life

Materials Needed

- writing paper
- pens, pencils
- art supplies
- Bible
- Lesson 8 Activity Masters

Call to Prayer

Loving God, you designed marriage to call a man and a woman to leave parents and cling to each other, becoming one. Let my students be touched by the beauty of your plan for spousal love. Let them listen to your call for their individual vocation in life. Amen.

Marriage and Family

LESSON 8

The Call to Love

John and his best man, Charlie, were pacing in the sacristy waiting for the wedding Mass to begin. Today was the day John had been waiting for all year. Today he and Joan would marry each other. John checked the mirror again. He looked fine.

"Relax," Charlie assured him, "Everything's going to be great."

John smiled back, "You're right. It's a perfect day. Charlie, do me a favor. Go find Joan and give her this note." He handed Charlie a small envelope.

Charlie found Joan near the church door. She stood with her brother, Mike, who was going to walk her up the aisle. Joan's dad had died several years ago. "You look great!" Charlie told Joan. She hugged him. Charlie was John's best friend, and Joan knew that the two of them would always be good friends. "So do you," she said.

Charlie gave Joan the note, and tried not to look curious about what it said. She opened the envelope, read the message, smiled, and showed it to Charlie. John had written just one word: "Forever."

During the wedding Mass, Charlie looked around the church. He saw his parents, who had just celebrated their thirtieth anniversary. There was Joan's mom, a widow. John's great-aunt, Sister Therese, was there too. She'd been a sister for more than 50 years. There was also Father Dan Dooley, who was presiding over the marriage.

The church was filled with people who had committed their lives to a variety of vocations, or callings from God to a particular way of life. Now John and Joan were about to promise to each other before Father Dan and all those in the church to accept and live God's call to the life-long vocation of marriage.

This lesson will help you to:

- **explore** that, in addition to marriage, there are a variety of vocations.
- **understand** the two purposes of marriage.
- **identify** ways that the Fruits of the Holy Spirit can guide family life.

To which vocations have people in your life made a commitment?

Teaching Tip

Annulments: The Catholic Church does not believe in divorce, but does have the practice of granting an annulment to certain failed marriages. An annulment declares the couple never achieved a truly sacramental marriage. Their "marriage" lacked certain essential qualities required by the Church. Individuals who have received annulments are free to later marry in the Church.

Objective

To recognize that marriage is but one vocation

Pray

Open the lesson with a prayer for marriage and family.

Focus

Invite students who have participated in or attended a wedding or Nuptial Mass to share their experiences with the class. Elicit details about the ritual and then discuss how these symbols and actions relate to marriage.

Discover

- Have students read "The Call to Love." Then have volunteers dramatize the story. Give special attention to their actions.
- Inquire: How do you think these characters felt in this event? Why do you think such an event is ritualized?
- Explain that major life events are ritualized to express their importance and to show respect and care for those involved.
- Point out the major vocations included in the story: married life (John and Joan), priesthood (Father Dan Dooley) religious life (Sister Therese) and single life (Joan's mom, who is now a widow).

Objective

To understand the two purposes of marriage

Focus

Have students read Mark 10:1–12. Explain that Jesus described God's plan for marriage. Moses did allow divorce, but God does not desire divorce. Yet God does not want anyone to stay in an unhealthy or abusive relationship. Jesus teaches the serious nature of marriage and why the state of a person's heart is important.

Explore

- Have students quietly read "Sharing the Gift of Life and Love."
- Read Catholics Believe. Discuss: In what ways is marriage a sign of God's love?
- Explain that in marriage a couple makes a promise of lifelong commitment and fidelity to each other. Inquire: Why is a lifelong commitment needed in marriage? Lifelong fidelity?
- Talk about the keeping of promises. When should a promise be kept? *(when freely given and leads to healthy growth)* When should a promise not be kept? *(when it is coerced by threat or fear; when keeping the promise may cause harm)*

Catholics Believe

Within marriage God's gift of love is fully expressed as a sign of the couple's unselfish, faithful love, and their openness to the creation of human life. By the graces of the Sacrament of Marriage and other Sacraments, the baptized married couple helps one another attain holiness.

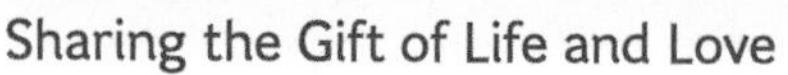

Sharing the Gift of Life and Love

Jesus, echoing the story of creation from the Book of Genesis, used this beautiful expression to describe marriage: "from the beginning of creation, 'God made them male and female. For this reason a man shall leave his father and mother [and be joined to his wife], and the two shall become one flesh.' So they are no longer two but one flesh. Therefore what God has joined together, no human being must separate" (Mark 10:6–9). God has willed that when a man and a woman marry they are to be permanently and faithfully committed to one another.

The relationship of marriage is fully expressed in the conjugal act of love in which husband and wife become "one flesh." The conjugal act of love is sexual intercourse in marriage. The pleasure, tenderness, and care a married couple show each other expresses and deepens their love and commitment. In their spousal love, husband and wife exclusively share the most intimate love through the complete giving of self to the other.

Think about the commitment necessary for love between spouses.

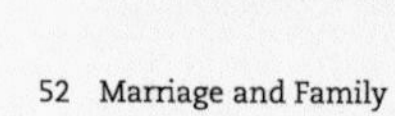

Sexual intercourse in marriage has two wonderful purposes. First, God made sexual intercourse pleasurable in order to help bond the married couple. In this way they grow closer by exploring, celebrating, and nurturing one another in a way that physically, emotionally, and spiritually unites them. This experience of being "one flesh" is a way of expressing with their whole body what they are saying with their whole life. That is, "I freely, faithfully, fully, and forever belong to you."

Second, God made sexual intercourse the way to cooperate with God in the creation of a new human being. When a married couple becomes parents (through conception, adoption, or fostering), they take on new responsibilities. In addition to their spousal love, they are now responsible for the love and care of

52 Marriage and Family

Teaching Tip

Natural Family Planning (NFP): There are various methods for regulating conception that reflect the moral and spiritual teachings of the Church. NFP can help a couple morally plan their family using God's plan for marriage. Detailed explanations of NFP should be avoided at this age since a full presentation would require a mature discussion of spousal tracking of the natural cycles of the female body. Female students, however, should learn and appreciate the beauty of their bodies and the amazing divine design of the reproductive system. Male students should also learn to appreciate God's design of their bodies and the responsible role of men in relationships.

their child. They provide the basic necessities of life to their children by providing a loving home, healthful foods, a good education, spiritual formation, and encouragement for life. In this way parents are important ministers within their family. Because of this new family, the Church refers to them as a domestic Church. The parents carry out God's work at home.

Sexual intercourse, then, is the complete giving of self as spouse and the openness to creating new life. This is why the Church teaches that sexual activity that is not open to new life or is not freely shared between husband and wife is not what God designed it to be. Thus any use of contraception, non-marital sex, and adultery are contrary to God's Law and the teachings of the Church.

Growing in Virtue

Fidelity, or **faithfulness,** is one of the essential ingredients for healthy relationships. The faithfulness between spouses is necessary for the indissoluble, life-giving bond and permanence of their love and the love they witness within their family.

"Thank You Note"

Write a short note to thank your parents or guardians for sharing God's gift of new life with you through conception, adoption, or fostering.

Activity

Extending the Lesson

Using Activity Master 8A: Use the Activity Master "A Message about Marriage." This activity is a fun opportunity for students to learn a key message about marriage: Successful marriage is always a triangle: a man, a woman and God.

Trust in Promises: Invite students to share experiences of making promises or demonstrating trust. Focus on the expectations of making a promise and the consequences of breaking them. Clearly explain different kinds of secrets. For example, keeping secret a surprise birthday party is not the same as keeping secret the mistreatment of someone. Discuss how students might react in situations where a promise was broken or a secret revealed for good and bad reasons.

- Using the previous lesson's list of qualities of a good friend, discuss why spouses need to be the closest of friends and deeply respect each other.
- Have students list the qualities of a healthy married couple. Be sure that their qualities point out "free, faithful, fully and forever" as necessary in the marriage. Then read the Growing in Virtue box.

Connect

- Discuss that commitment in marriage helps spouses become parents. Ask: How is parenting a ministry? *(God relies on parents to raise their children to know and love him.)*
- Explain that God's plan for spouses to be open to life includes having children through natural conception, adoption and/or fostering.
- Have students complete the activity on the page. Explain that when we give thanks, we show respect and can encourage others to do the same.
- Time permitting, ask: Why is contraception contrary to God's plan for marriage? Explain that its mentality involves a lack of openness to God's plan for marriage. Marriage is to involve generous love between spouses and openness to serving life in marriage.

APPLY

Objective

To explore how the Fruits of the Holy Spirit guide family life

Focus

Read the Catholic Family Album box. Ask: How was Blessed Zélie Martin a role model for women? *(Despite terrible hardship, she remained loyal and loving as a wife to Louis and a mother to her children.)*

Discover

- Have students read Galatians 5:13–26. Explain that Saint Paul too here is concerned about the state of a person's heart and our need for God's grace to help guide us in our actions.
- Inquire: How does God help you in choosing to do what is good and avoiding what is evil?

Integrate

- Read the text on the page. Respond to any questions students may have about the activity on the page.
- Have students complete the activity on the page. Then share as a class examples of each.

Pray

Pray for the intercession of Blessed Zélie and Blessed Louis Martin to inspire us in family life.

Catholic Family Album

Blessed Zélie Martin and her husband, **Blessed Louis,** are the parents of Saint Thérèse of Lisieux (Thérèse of the Child Jesus) and three other children. Zelie gave birth to four children, but three others died prior to being born. She was strong in her faith and passionate about life. Tragically, Zélie died when Thérèse was four-and-half years old. She had deeply influenced all of her children. When Pope John Paul II began the process of the canonization of Zelie and Louis, they became the first married couple considered to be named Saints. They are honored by the Catholic Church as exemplary parents.

Witnessing Christian Love

One of the perhaps more frustrating things about being a parent is that just when you feel like you're good at it, your children have grown up.

The raising of a child is a commitment to charity, patience, and generosity. These qualities are three of the twelve Fruits of the Holy Spirit. The others are joy, peace, kindness, goodness, gentleness, faithfulness, modesty, self-control, and chastity. The Fruits of the Holy Spirit are signs of God's work in one's life, or in any relationship, including family life.

In the space below, choose three or more of the Fruits of the Holy Spirit and give an example from life in which you have witnessed each lived out. Then describe one way you can give witness to it in your friendships or family now.

Fruit of the Holy Spirit: ____________

How I see it at work: ____________

What I will do to give witness to it: ____________

Fruit of the Holy Spirit: ____________

How I see it at work: ____________

What I will do to give witness to it: ____________

Fruit of the Holy Spirit: ____________

How I see it at work: ____________

What I will do to give witness to it: ____________

54 Marriage and Family

Extending the Lesson

Using Activity Master 8B: Use the Activity Master "A Community of Love." This activity helps students to reflect on Romans 12:9–12 by addressing the qualities of love and acts of love.

Commandments for Parents: Invite students to write a list of parents' instructions. The list should include the top ten things a parent needs to know or do in their ministry of raising their family as a domestic Church. The list can be based on the Ten Commandments, the Beatitudes or the Fruits of the Holy Spirit. Have them discuss and amend the list with parents. Then have the youth and their parents sign it as a joint commitment to their family.

Activity Master 8A

Name

A Message about Marriage

Use the Code Key to decipher the hidden message about marriage. Do you think the message applies to every marriage? Why or why not?

Code Key

26=A	13=N
25=B	12=O
24=C	11=P
23=D	10=Q
22=E	9=R
21=F	8=S
20=G	7=T
19=H	6=U
18=I	5=V
17=J	4=W
16=K	3=X
15=L	2=Y
14=M	1=Z

The Message

S U C C E S S F U L
8 6 24 24 22 8 8 21 6 15

M A R R I A G E
14 26 9 9 18 26 20 22

I S A L W A Y S
18 8 26 15 4 26 2 8

A T R I A N G L E:
26 7 9 18 26 13 20 15 22

A M A N, A W O M A N,
26 14 26 13 26 4 12 14 26 13

A N D G O D.
26 13 23 20 12 23

Family Life Grade 8

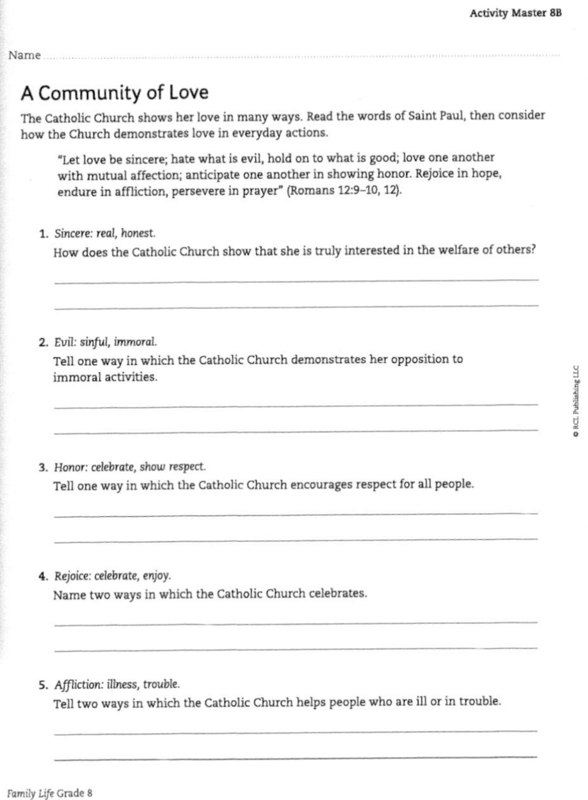

Activity Master 8B

Name

A Community of Love

The Catholic Church shows her love in many ways. Read the words of Saint Paul, then consider how the Church demonstrates love in everyday actions.

"Let love be sincere; hate what is evil, hold on to what is good; love one another with mutual affection; anticipate one another in showing honor. Rejoice in hope, endure in affliction, persevere in prayer" (Romans 12:9–10, 12).

1. *Sincere: real, honest.*
   How does the Catholic Church show that she is truly interested in the welfare of others?
2. *Evil: sinful, immoral.*
   Tell one way in which the Catholic Church demonstrates her opposition to immoral activities.
3. *Honor: celebrate, show respect.*
   Tell one way in which the Catholic Church encourages respect for all people.
4. *Rejoice: celebrate, enjoy.*
   Name two ways in which the Catholic Church celebrates.
5. *Affliction: illness, trouble.*
   Tell two ways in which the Catholic Church helps people who are ill or in trouble.

Family Life Grade 8

How to Find It
How to Use It

Step 1: Click & Select

Go to RCLBFamilyLife.com
Click on the link for activities.
Then select the activity master you need.

Step 2: Print & Copy

Print each activity master in advance.
Then copy enough for everyone in the class.

Step 3: Share & Discuss

Once students have completed the activity, have them share and discuss their responses.

REVIEWING UNIT 4

Summary

- Ask the students to read through the Summary section.
- Invite them to ask questions about any points that are not clear to them.
- Make sure to expand on any points that were perhaps touched on only lightly during class time.

Thinking It Through

- Have students answer all three questions on the page.
- Assign each student a number from one through three.
- Have students share with the class their answer to the question that corresponds to their assigned number.

Matching It Up

Use this matching section to help the students identify the appropriate definition or description of a key concept, term or person from the unit.

REVIEWING UNIT 4

Name ....

Summary

Remember what you have learned in each of the lessons in God's Gift of Love.

LESSON 7: Loving Together

- Developing and deepening friendships can be preparation for the lifelong commitment of marriage and parenting.
- Human sexuality is primarily concerned with our capacity to love and form relationships based on being male or female.
- Self-knowledge and self-preservation are two key aspects of modesty that are necessary for healthy friendships.

LESSON 8: Marriage and Family

- Married love is to be self-giving and life-giving.
- God provides grace to the married couple through the Sacrament of Matrimony so that they can freely, faithfully, fully, and forever love one another.
- Christian parenting requires living out the Fruits of the Holy Spirit.

Thinking It Through

1. How is it possible for boys and girls to be friends?

2. How do you define true Christian love?

3. What are the benefits a married couple receives in the Sacrament of Matrimony?

Matching It Up

On each line, write the letter of the description in Column B that best goes with the term in Column A.

A

1. ...B... Courting
2. ...E... Contraception
3. ...A... Modesty
4. ...C... Sexuality
5. ...D... Vocation

B

A. Holding on to and guarding the sacredness of the body through proper speech, attire, and conduct

B. The social practice of seeking and acquiring a spouse that has changed over the years

C. Human capacity to love and form relationships based on gender

D. A calling from God to a particular state of life

E. A mentality and a practice contrary to God's plan for marriage

REVIEWING UNIT 4

Name..

Recalling Key Concepts

Circle the T if the statement is true. Circle the F if the statement is false.

1. The practice of dating has not changed in over two hundred years. T (F)
2. Through her teachings, the Catholic Church promotes and preserves God's plan for marriage. (T) F
3. Sex outside of marriage violates the dignity of marriage. (T) F
4. Dating between teens today is great practice for marriage. T (F)
5. Parenting from a Christian perspective is a ministry. (T) F

Fill in the missing words in these sentences.

6. The ......LIFE-GIVING...... purpose of marriage is how the married couple cooperates with God in the creation of a new human being.
7. Developing and deepening ......FRIENDSHIP...... is one of the best ways to prepare for the commitment required of marriage.
8. The ......SELF-GIVING...... purpose of marriage helps the married couple become closer by exploring, celebrating, and nurturing one another in a way that physically, emotionally and spiritually unites them.
9. The attitude of self-respect and the practice of ......SELF-KNOWLEDGE...... are how we learn more about ourselves through the experiences of being in relationships.
10. The practice of ......MODESTY...... is one important way we learn to preserve our integrity in relationships.

Working Together

In small groups, investigate safe, inexpensive, and fun places to go and things to do for young teens in groups in your area. After you have completed your research, create a directory that you can share with the whole class.

56 Unit 4 Review

Teaching Tip

Journal Activity: Take one of the questions in Thinking It Through and invite students to write their response in a journal. Suggest to students that they can respond to the question by sketching a picture, writing poetry or prose or making lyrics to a simple song. Encourage creative writing in their journal activity. Time permitting, invite volunteers to share what they wrote or sketched.

Recalling Key Concepts

- Use this section to help the students be able to accurately recall the key concepts from the unit.
- For the true and false section, you can have students correct any false statements.
- To help with the fill-in-the-blank section, you might want to provide a word bank on the board.

Working Together

- Choose a project that best fits the needs and abilities of your students, as well as your time schedule.
- Time permitting, have students complete the unit assessment individually or as a class; otherwise, encourage them to complete it at home.

UNIT 5

God's Gift of Community

Background

"The family is the place of origin and the most effective means for humanizing and personalizing society: it makes an original contribution in depth to building up the world, by making possible a life that is, properly speaking, human, in particular by guarding and transmitting virtues and 'values' " (Familiaris Consortio *43).*

WE ARE CREATED TO LOVE AND BE LOVED. THERE IS a basic human need to belong. We find the fulfillment of this need through belonging to family, school, Church, civic community, the workplace and many other groups. As humans, we are social beings. We find our deepest happiness in experiencing and sharing life with others. We are created to love and be loved.

Some have called us "a nation of strangers." With high mobility of individuals and families, some feeling of being alone is understandable. Still, we do well to affirm our need for others and their need for us. Hard though it may be, we are to constantly fight against excessive individualism.

THE SEARCH FOR BELONGING AMONG THE YOUTH is highlighted by the influence, both positive and negative, of their peers. Young people need to be aware of the influence of their peers in the choices of friends and groups. They can choose positive forms of belonging, such as school clubs and teams, church youth groups and choir, community dance and theater groups and other civic organizations that reach out and work with people in need. But they can also be influenced to choose negative forms of belonging, such as gangs or cliques. What these choices have in common is that both positive and negative forms of community attract their members because they offer acceptance, protection, identity, support—they provide a sense of belonging.

AS THE FAMILY GOES, SO GOES THE WORLD. FAMILY and friends have an irreplaceable role in our lives. All of us are called by God to a generosity of spirit. We are led by the Holy Spirit to reach out to others and share in the bounty that God has provided. As we plan our future, no matter what our age, we are to serve the many needs of the world. We are each other's keepers.

Families can serve the needs of others in a variety of ways. There are school and Church service projects that can also be family projects. The home is not a place to store and protect your possessions. It is to be a place of hospitality where others are welcomed and where the needs of others can be addressed. The responsibility of responding to the needs of others knows no borders or boundaries. "In a global culture driven by excessive individualism, our tradition proclaims that the person is not only sacred but also social. How we organize our society . . . directly affects human dignity and the capacity of individuals to grow in community" *(Sharing Catholic Social Teaching: Challenges and Directions, "Major Themes").*

Additional Background

Catechism of the Catholic Church: §§ 946–962, 1877, 1906, 1912–1916, 1925–1926

If you are a teacher, you are given abundant opportunities to share of yourself. The classroom or the learning center is a holy place where those gathered can become more conscious of their place and responsibilities in this wonderful world God has given us.

For Reflection

Read and reflect on the following:

"[T]he Catholic tradition teaches that human beings grow and achieve fulfillment in community" (Sharing Catholic Social Teaching: Challenges and Directions, "Major Themes").

- How does my belonging to the Church, the community of believers in Jesus Christ, affect the way I participate in my family and other communities?
- What expectations might I establish that guide the young people to participate as responsible members of our "class community"?

Child Safety

Online social networks create new challenges in the effort to keep children safe. Sexual predators can easily prey upon the unsuspecting person as they chat blithely away with "friends." Lesson 9 introduces social networking safety tips and provides an opportunity for the students to discuss this topic and to determine acceptable behaviors. Lesson 10 addresses the question of appropriate responsibility for eighth-graders.

Family Focus

Families can serve the needs of others in many ways. There are service projects that can also be family projects. The home should not be a place to store and protect your possessions, but rather a place of hospitality where others can be welcomed and the needs of others can be addressed. Invite the parents of your students to use the Family Time pages and the Parent Connection to discuss the family's role in serving the needs of the community.

UNIT 5

God's Gift of Community

Family Time

You Are Not Alone

Family Blessings

Healthy Habits in the Home

Making Connections

Faith on the Fridge

LESSON 9 PLANNER

Goal: To learn ways of choosing groups to belong to and identify the qualities of a good role model

Engage
Page 97

Objective
To appreciate the benefits of belonging to a community

Family Time
Ensure that each student tears out their Family Time page to complete at home.

Pray
Prayer for community

Focus
Group building activity

Discover
Discuss the importance of solidarity within groups.

Teach
Page 98

Objective
To understand the importance of choosing friends and role models

Focus
Evaluate the positive influence of their groups.

Explore
Read, discuss and summarize the importance of the kinds of groups with whom we associate and their influences in our lives.
Growing in Virtue: Vigilance
Catholics Believe: Community enriches our lives.

Connect
Describe a good role model

Apply
Page 100

Objective
To identify social skills necessary for healthy relationships

Focus
Catholic Family Album: Saint John Bosco

Discover
Identify values and virtues in given situations.

Integrate
Assess personal social skills.

Pray
Prayer for intercession of Saint John Bosco

Vocabulary Preview

Cliques—social groups formed to exclude others; often this results in the harassment of those excluded

Gangs—social groups formed around criminal activity often dealing with vandalism, drugs, robbery or murder

Solidarity—a sense of unity and belonging with another or within a group of people

Social Networking—an online phenomenon where people are increasingly forming social groups or friends

Vigilance—an attitude and skill of being alert and watchful of a person's surroundings and interaction with others

Materials Needed

- writing paper
- pens, pencils
- art supplies
- Bible
- toothpicks and string
- Lesson 9 Activity Masters

Call to Prayer

Lord, many pressures and temptations can lead us into harmful social associations. Help my students see the importance of choosing their friends and activities wisely. Give me the wisdom to speak honestly and prudently. Amen.

The Social Scene

We Belong to One Another

Jeanne shivered and it was not just because the house was cold this winter night. As she sat with her family trying to watch television, Jeanne couldn't help feeling scared. She listened intently to the sound of every passing car. Her attention wandered from the television to the window where her family had put a lighted menorah.

Two nights ago, on the first night of Hanukkah, the eight-day Jewish festival, rocks and bricks had been thrown through the windows of Jewish homes in Jeanne's town. People were hurt. Posters and flyers had appeared all over town threatening harm to people. The posters were promoting violence against Jews, African Americans, and others.

The police and other town officials advised Jewish families to remove their menorahs from their windows so gang members couldn't target their homes. But before the menorahs could be taken down, something remarkable happened. Menorahs started appearing in windows all over town. Pictures of menorahs were also displayed in shop windows. Even Christian churches displayed menorahs. In Jeanne's Catholic parish, St. Bernard, families were contacted by phone asking them to display menorahs in solidarity with their Jewish neighbors. Jeanne's family talked it over and agreed to do so.

Despite Jeanne's nervousness, no assaults were made against her family or the rest of the town. The eight days of Hanukkah gave police enough time to identify and arrest some of the gang members responsible. Those eight days gave everyone in the town a chance to learn what it means to belong to a wonderful community.

This lesson will help you to:

- **explore** and appreciate the benefits of belonging to a community.
- **understand** the importance of choosing friends and role models.
- **identify** and put into practice social skills to improve relationships.

In what ways do you feel connected to your local community and your parish community?

Teaching Tip

Peer Pressure: As young children enter adolescence, the influence of their family often gives way to the social influences of their peer groups. Sometimes peer pressure can be positive, but it also exerts a negative influence. This negative influence can lack any moral sensitivity. It can also be very egocentric in its short-sightedness. As you discuss in this lesson the concepts of solidarity, vigilance and community, encourage your students to evaluate the benefits of belonging to their particular groups. While loyalty to friends is to be admired, it never should be a reason to stay in potentially harmful or hurtful situations.

ENGAGE

Objective

To appreciate the benefits of belonging to a community

Pray

Open the lesson with a prayer thanking God for community.

Focus

Place students in groups and give each group 10 toothpicks and a 6-foot piece of string. Have each group construct the most solid and sturdy structure they can in two minutes. Compare the final results of each group.

Discover

- Have students discuss their experience of their group work, especially how it impacted the results of their efforts. Note that the sturdiest are those that bundle sticks together. Compare the solidity of their structures to the idea of strength in numbers. There is safety in numbers. Have students give examples for this axiom.

- Have students read, "We Belong to One Another." Check to see what they know about Hanukkah. Add details the youth do not include.
- Inquire: How would you define "solidarity"? Explain that it is the sense of unity in belonging to others and the sharing of material and spiritual blessings.
- Discuss students' feelings of connectedness to their school, parish and family.
- Discuss the saying "You cannot build up yourself by tearing down another."

TEACH

Objective

To understand the importance of choosing friends and role models

Focus

- Have students list the kinds of groups to which they belong; for example, family, school, parish, neighborhood, etc.
- Direct the youth to evaluate each of the groups they named by asking which one: (1) is most helpful in their growth; (2) not sure they want to continue to be in; (3) is most valuable to them. Elicit reasons for their responses.

Explore

- Have students quietly read "The Right Companions." Allow for students to react and ask questions.
- Discuss what students believe are some reasons why people join cliques and gangs. Inquire: How else can these reasons be satisfied in other groups without joining a negative kind of group?
- Read "Social Networking" allowing for questions and comments.
- Ask students how they use social networks. Together, make a list of the benefits of these networks. Then, make a list of concerns they have about them.

Growing in Virtue

Prudence and **fortitude** are Cardinal Moral Virtues that help us develop friendships. They help us be vigilant in forming friendships and joining groups. Real friends help us to be a better person. They can help us choose what is good.

The Right Companions

People naturally need and want to belong. We belong to our family and to other groups outside of family. This natural desire to belong and to fit in with others is a strong influence in every person's life.

Members of a group influence the group, and the group influences its members. This influence, or peer pressure, can be good or bad. When peer pressure gives you the courage to stand up for what is right, like in Jeanne's situation, the members become more united, and the group is stronger.

You are old enough now to make choices about developing friendships and belonging to groups. Recall that God created you to live in relationships. This is why everyone enjoys having friends. You and your friends will naturally form groups of friends. These friends can be supportive in seeking what is good and doing what is right, or they can have a hurtful or harmful influence on your choices.

Think about the groups you belong to and their influence upon you.

Social Networking

Our desire for having friends and belonging to others is so strong that we can even seek a sense of belonging in a "virtual" way. In other words, we may try to connect with others even if we have never met them in person. Today the Internet provides many people the chance to connect with their friends and join groups online. Connecting with friends and others via the Internet is called online social networking.

Unfortunately, there are some people who abuse the use of social networking. Therefore, each of us needs to be vigilant in using the Internet. Vigilance is not being paranoid. It is about being aware of and alert regarding your surroundings and your actions. We all need to be careful of what we communicate and with whom we communicate. It is important to avoid using social networking to abuse others. We need to especially avoid cyber-bullying.

60 The Social Scene

Teaching Tip

Tips for Safe Online Social Networking

These rules will help your students safely network online:

Protect your personal information. Never post information that could help a stranger identify you or where you live.

Choose your screen name carefully. Don't give people clues on how to find you.

Be circumspect. Remember that everything you post could be seen by anyone for years to come.

Use care when adding "friends." People online may hide behind false identities.

Stop communicating with anyone you meet online who wants to meet in person. Tell your parents or other trusted adults about this request.

Check a site's privacy policy. Don't use sites that share your information with others.

TEACH

As a young person, you are in the process of establishing your own identity. In this process you may join various groups. You need to be vigilant about not joining groups that routinely bring harm to their own members and others.

Teens also regularly choose role models. A role model is someone you admire and want to be like. They might be a sports figure, a musician, a celebrity, a family member, or an older student in your school. Our Church family, both living members and members who have died, is filled with many role models. They model for us practical ways to treat others with respect, with justice, and with love. They model for us ways of becoming the person God created us to be. Examine who your role models are right now. Examine why you chose these people. Look carefully to see how well they model for you ways to grow in love and responsibility as a follower of Jesus Christ.

Catholics Believe

Love of neighbor and love of God are inseparable. Being part of a community enriches our lives. Solidarity builds friendships and community. Solidarity is the just and generous sharing of all our gifts, material and spiritual. Each of us develops our potential through service, communication, and being with one another.

A Good Role Model

Write a short description of a person you consider to be a good role model. They can be from history or living now.

- Review the rules their parents have established for using these networks. Work with the students to create what they think would be appropriate rules for eighth graders. What is important here is the discussion that takes place.
- Emphasize the 3 Rs of child safety: Recognize, Respond, Report. Also review the rules on proper boundaries, appropriate friendships, and how to ask for help.

- Have students read the Growing in Virtue box on the previous page. Have them list examples of being vigilant while online.
- Challenge students to identify the top three qualities that they look for in a good role model. Discuss as a class.
- Read the Catholics Believe box. Inquire: How does being with someone help deepen a relationship with God? Use the example of service projects or mission trips.

Connect

- Have students complete the activity on the page. Explain that the activity is more about listing the characteristics and values of a role model.
- Discuss the various role models identified as a class. Be sure to identify role models for all aspects of life: physical, mental, emotional and spiritual.
- Time permitting, have students discuss how they can be or are role models for younger students in their school or parish, or for a younger brother or sister or cousin.

Extending the Lesson

Using Activity Master 9A: Use the Activity Master "Positive and Negative Peers." This activity helps students to identify signs of a positive peer or a negative peer. Then, students will explore best practices of being involved with a group of friends.

Hall of Fame: Have students create a "Role Model Hall of Fame" in the classroom. Establish as a class the criteria needed for someone to be inducted. Suggest that criteria reflect a certain core set of values and attributes necessary for achieving a happy, healthy and holy life. In order for a person to be inducted, a simple majority vote can be the easiest way and the class can induct as many individuals as they like.

APPLY

Objective

To identify social skills necessary for healthy relationships

Focus

Read the Catholic Family Album box. Inquire: Why do you think Saint John Bosco is a good role model?

Discover

- Have students respond to the following: What do you do when: (1) a new student comes to the lunch room; (2) you promise to help out after dinner; (3) a neighbor offers to give you a ride home; (4) a friend is failing a subject you excel in.
- Challenge students to identify the possible value each of these virtues contributes to a healthy relationship: (1) hospitality, (2) commitment, (3) safety, (4) compassion.
- Review with students when it is inappropriate to keep a commitment. (When the commitment is forced or may cause or allow harm.)

Integrate

- Read the text on the page. Make sure students understand each skill.
- Have them complete the activity on the page. Then share as a class examples of each.

Pray

Pray for the intercession of Saint John Bosco for a deeper appreciation of the good friends we have.

Catholic Family Album

Saint John Bosco worked during the mid-1800s to help homeless boys living on the streets of Turin, Italy. He gave them food, clothing, shelter, education, and a way out of their dead-end life of crime and violence. During much of his life, John focused on the religious education of children by teaching them and by writing books on how to teach children. By teaching them trade skills, he provided the youth with skills they could use to improve their own lives. Today the Salesians, the religious orders of men and of women founded by Saint John Bosco, work with street kids and other at-risk young people all over the world.

Practicing Social Skills

Getting along with others requires the effort to name and practice social skills. These skills, which help you to be both a dependable and responsible member of your family and also a good friend, will also help you be a welcomed and valued member of any group or community.

Here is a list of several social skills. Give an example of how each skill can help you get along with others. Then choose the skill you think that you need to develop the most. Write down one way that you will practice that skill this week.

Commitment gives you the ability to keep your promises. ____________________

Communication is founded on openness and honesty in speech and action. ____________________

Affirmation results in helping others feel good about themselves. ____________________

Compromise is the skill of solving problems so everyone wins. ____________________

Patience allows us to work for long-term goals, even if it means postponing personal gratification. ____________________

Trust means you can depend on others and they can depend on you. ____________________

A sense of humor helps keep small irritations from becoming big problems. ____________________

The skill I need to work on most is: ____________________

Something I will do to practice this skill: ____________________

Extending the Lesson

Using Activity Master 9B: Use the Activity Master "Role Models from Your Faith Family." This activity helps students examine the qualities of a good role model and identify those qualities most admired.

Evaluating Groups: Have students list the specific groups to which they belong. Then have them identify the social skills they can practice within each of those groups. On a continuum have them then evaluate how effective or helpful each group is in aiding them on being able to practice those social skills. Use this activity to guide students in discerning the importance and value of the groups with whom they associate or belong.

ONLINE ACTIVITIES FOR LESSON 9

Activity Master 9A

Name ....

Positive and Negative Peers

How can you spot positive and negative peers? How can you be your best if you're part of a group? Read each section, add your own ideas, and share them with a partner.

Signs of the Positive Peer

- A positive peer respects your beliefs.
- A positive peer is democratic.
- A positive peer won't ask you to do something that makes you uncomfortable.

A positive peer ________________________________

A positive peer ________________________________

Signs of the Negative Peer

- A negative peer doesn't care what your principles are.
- A negative peer's friendship is based on your always going along with what he or she wants to do.
- A negative peer puts down people outside of his or her own group.

A positive peer ________________________________

A positive peer ________________________________

Being Your Best in a Group

- Don't always wait for others in the group to decide what to do; express your own opinions.
- Make friends outside your group, and try some new activities.

What could you do if your group started getting into something you were uncomfortable with?

____

____

____

____

____

____

Family Life Grade 8

Activity Master 9B

Name ....

Role Models from Your Faith Family

No one can be exactly like another person. But you can try on the best qualities of people you respect. Write down the qualities you most admire in each of these people from your Faith Family.

Jesus

Imagine the qualities it took to leave home and a secure life to tell people about a new way of life. Jesus had unconventional friends, and gave His best to everyone. He risked persecution of His beliefs.

Qualities I admire in Jesus:

____

____

Saint Teresa of Avila

Teresa was devoted to God, but her life was not all silence and solemnity. She led her nuns in observing strict rules of poverty and obedience, but also led them in dancing with castanets on feast days.

Qualities I admire in Saint Teresa:

____

____

Saint Don Bosco

"Singing, shouting, scabrous slum boys" is what people called the tough kids Don Bosco took in. "Bosco is mad," said others. But Saint Don Bosco turned the boys' lives around with his love and respect.

Qualities I admire in Saint Don Bosco:

____

____

1. Choose a role model from your present-day Faith Family, and name two qualities you most admire in him or her.
2. Of all the qualities you've named above, circle those that you would most like to make part of your own life.

Family Life Grade 8

How to Find It
How to Use It

Step 1: Click & Select

Go to RCLBFamilyLife.com
Click on the link for activities.
Then select the activity master you need.

Step 2: Print & Copy

Print each activity master in advance.
Then copy enough for everyone in the class.

Step 3: Share & Discuss

Once students have completed the activity, have them share and discuss their responses.

LESSON 10 PLANNER

Goal: To reflect on our past to appreciate the growth experienced and anticipate the future maturity as we seek meaning and purpose in life

Engage
Page 103

Objective
To assess past experiences as readiness for the future

Pray
Prayer for family

Focus
Share past experiences with family members.

Discover
Identify examples of growth in all areas.

Teach
Page 104

Objective
To understand how aspects of our lives give meaning and purpose

Focus
Share experiences of passages.

Explore
Read, discuss and summarize the importance of responsibility in all areas of life and how it is a sign of maturity and readiness.
Growing in Virtue: Responsibility and wisdom
Catholics Believe: God's plan for human life

Connect
Design a bumper sticker or button.

Apply
Page 106

Objective
To make choices to use our resources in healthy ways

Focus
Catholic Family Album: Saint Hildegard von Bingen

Discover
Brainstorm an action plan to attain a dream.

Integrate
Reflect on what it will be like in the future.

Pray
Intercessory Prayer

Reviewing Unit 5
Summarize and review the content from both lessons.

Vocabulary Preview

Responsibility—quality of being dependable or accountable for one's attitudes, decisions and actions,

Materials Needed

- writing paper
- pens, pencils
- art supplies
- Bible
- Lesson 10 Activity Masters

Call to Prayer

Lord, as this series comes to an end, strengthen me with the energy and enthusiasm to help my students see meaning and purpose in their lives. Give them the hope and strength to continue reaching for possibilities that God will place before them. Amen.

Growing in Christ

A Whole New World

"I wonder what she's thinking," Patricia said, as she looked into the big brown eyes of her niece, Christine. Patricia's sister Margie laughed as she took the squirming baby back. "She's probably thinking just what you did when you were two weeks old," Margie said. " 'Is it time to eat yet?' " Patricia shook her head. She couldn't even imagine what it was like to be that little.

"You were all that little once," Grandma Ricco said, looking around the room filled with relatives. The whole family had gathered to celebrate Christine's Baptism.

Patricia sat by herself in a corner for a little while, thinking, "I can't even imagine what it was like for me when I was a baby." Patricia was the tallest girl in her eighth-grade class and the captain of the volleyball team. Looking at Margie she thought, "I wonder what I will be like when I am as old as Margie? And what will it be like to be a grandmother?" Patricia had never stopped to think about her past and future before.

Your childhood years are behind you, and your years of adolescence are soon upon you. You've conquered challenges and come through each of them a little wiser. You are beginning to sort out the complicated emotions of puberty. You're forming friendships, learning to be loyal to others. You're finding out more and more how important it is to be close to Christ and part of the Church.

Gradually, you are thinking about your future. Many of the things you are doing now are preparing you for one of the adult commitments in life: for marriage, the religious life, the single life, or for priesthood.

This lesson will help you to:

- **reflect** on the past as you look forward to the future.
- **discover** experiences in life that give Christian meaning and purpose.
- **dream** about your future contributions to society.

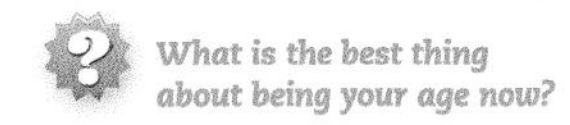

What is the best thing about being your age now?

Teaching Tip

Inner Clock: Keep in mind that the onset of puberty is determined by each student's inner clock, and no two young people will develop at the same rate or in the same way. Young adolescents whose growth is earlier or later than others in their class tend to be extremely uncomfortable. This can result in feelings of awkwardness and even feeling abnormal. All students need to be reminded that they will each grow at their own rate and in their own time. You may want to share the following information with students: during puberty most teens will gain about 50% of their adult body weight; between the ages of ten and sixteen, girls can grow up to nine inches and boys us to ten inches in height. We do well to marvel at God's great gift of life and how each of us develops and matures at our own pace.

Objective

To assess past experiences as readiness for the future

Pray

Open the lesson with a prayer thanking God for our families.

Focus

In three to five minutes have students write the names and ages of as many of their family members as possible. Then have them share one great moment they had with three people on their list.

Discover

- Have students read "A Whole New World." Inquire whether any students feel like Patricia in the story.
- Write on the board the four areas of human growth: physical, intellectual, emotional and spiritual.
- Invite students to write one concrete example of how they have grown in each area. Then have them share their responses with a partner to see what they have in common.
- Time permitting, have students compare what they remember about themselves when they were in first grade and compare who they are now with who they were then. Discuss as a class.

TEACH

Objective

To understand how aspects of our lives give meaning and purpose

Focus

- Invite volunteers to share with the class an experience of "passage" of themselves or someone they know; for example, taking first steps or words; riding a bike; graduation; marriage; driver's license; voting; going to college; etc.
- Discuss how some of these events of passage are celebrated. Explore the meanings of some of the rituals and symbols involved.

Explore

- Have students quietly read the text on the page. Point out that responsibility includes being held accountable for one's actions.
- Have students read the Growing in Virtue box. Discuss how wisdom and the Gifts of the Holy Spirit relate to fulfilling one's responsibilities.
- Place students in four groups, each with one area of responsibility. Each group is to report the meaning of their responsibility and to identify a concrete way an eighth grader might fulfill it as they mature.
- Have each group report to the class their responses and list them on the board.

Growing in Virtue

Wisdom is one of the seven Gifts of the Holy Spirit. This gift helps us see ourselves, others, and all creation "through the eyes of God." Wisdom gives us the ability learn more about the meaning and mystery of life. Wisdom helps us take on more responsibility for our physical, mental, emotional, and spiritual growth.

The Meaning of Life

You are experiencing and taking part in a stage of life that is part of growing up, or maturing. Part of maturing is taking more and more personal responsibility for your life. This does not mean you go it alone. Your parents, other family members, teachers, and the Church still have a vital role in helping guide you. It means that in certain areas of your life you must now take a little more initiative and responsibility. This includes seeking the advice of trusted adults who love and care for you and have your best interests in mind. Remember, they too experienced what you are experiencing now.

You are growing in responsibility in many areas of your life. This includes responsibilities in the physical, mental, emotional, and spiritual dimensions of your life.

Physical responsibility means treating your body and the bodies of others with proper respect and care. It means using your physical skills in a positive and virtuous way.

Mental responsibility means learning as much as you can and opening your mind to the knowledge that you will need as you grow older. It also means using your mind to learn ways to make good and wise choices.

Emotional responsibility means listening to your feelings and to those of others. It includes learning to share, cooperate, love, and forgive. Practicing self-control and being accountable for your actions are signs of deepening responsibility and maturity.

Spiritual responsibility means recognizing your dependence on God. By working hard on your relationship with Jesus and taking part as an active member of the Church, you can grow in wisdom and love.

Think about how you have grown in all of your responsibilities.

Finding meaning in life does not guarantee that you will have all the answers on your fingertips all the time. There will be days when nothing makes sense. Part of growing to real maturity is understanding that life includes mystery.

64 Growing in Christ

Teaching Tip

Six Ways to Show That You Are Responsible

1. *Do what you agree to do.* People learn to trust you when you keep your commitments. They doubt you when you don't.
2. *Stand up for your own actions.* Don't make excuses or blame others for what you did.
3. *Take care of your own things.* Take charge of your own life. Don't wait for others to remind you of what you are to do.
4. *Be someone others can trust.* Treat other's belongings with care and return what you borrow. Don't gossip or repeat what others tell you. Let people know that they can count on you.
5. *Think before you act.* Gather information, think it through and then do what is right.
6. *Don't procrastinate.* After you've decided what you should do, act on it. Don't put things off until later.

For Christians, this mystery is at the heart of our faith, our hope, and our love. One key to the mystery of life is knowing that you were created for a reason. God has created you to share in his life and love, now and forever. God, your family, and friends have given you love. Now it is your turn to share that love with others.

Every choice you make should reflect your purpose in life. Every person you meet offers an opportunity for you to share your love. You are a good and valuable person. You'll make mistakes, but if you keep the meaning and purpose in life at heart, you can and will do good. When you honor the deepest desire that God has placed in your heart, you are living the "good life." You will give yourself the best opportunities for meaning, freedom, joy, and love.

Catholics Believe

Life has meaning and our lives have purpose. God calls each of us to seek him, to know him, and to love him with all of our heart, mind, and strength. God gathers us together to be united as the one Family of God, the Church.

"Purpose in Life"

Design a button to share with others your purpose in life. Then reflect in prayer, asking God to help you continue to mature in love.

Extending the Lesson

Using Activity Master 10A: Use the Activity Master "Growth and Responsibility." This activity helps students to recognize the major growth and changes they have experienced since infancy.

Celebrating Passages: Invite students to plan ahead a life passage event that they will soon embark on: graduation from middle school or junior high school. Ask them to create a celebration to honor their achievements. Tell them that they can incorporate activities and symbols that are already associated with the celebration. Or they can find new ways to make it personal for them. Have the youth share their ideas with you. Gather their appropriate ideas and share them with the principal.

- Ask: What is an appropriate level of responsibility for an eighth grader? What should they be responsible for? *(their own attitudes, choices, actions, thoughts and behaviors)* What should they not be responsible for? *(the choices, thoughts, actions, attitudes and behaviors of others; others' problems)*
- Remind students that they are loved by God and that they can never lose that love.
- Read the Catholics Believe box. Discuss how involvement in their parish can lead them to be responsible in other areas.

Connect

- Engage students in a discussion that challenges them to defend their idea of the meaning of life, based on the content of this lesson.
- Inquire: What would you say to someone who says that life has no meaning?
- Have students complete the activity on the page. You might suggest the following Scripture as inspiration: John 13:34; I Corinthians 13; James 1:27; I John 2:10, 4:8; I Peter 4:8.
- Time permitting, have students identify practical ways that they can show they are responsible disciples of Jesus and members of the Church.

APPLY

Objective

To examine dreams and identify steps to attain them

Focus

Read the Catholic Family Album box. Inquire: How do you think God helped Saint Hildegard fulfill her dreams? *(Her visions might have been a way to encourage her.)*

Discover

- Pair-up students to share a personal dream of theirs. Note that it can be a dream that is unrealistic or possible. Have students brainstorm a plan of what it might take to make their dream come true.
- Invite a few volunteers to share with the class a plan to fulfill their dream. Explain that hurdles and changes are inevitable but keeping focus is part of the challenge too.

Integrate

- Read "Creating the Future You" aloud as a class. Make sure students understand the activity.
- Have students complete the activity on the page. Then share as a class examples of each.

Pray

Pray for the intercession of Saint Hildegard von Bingen or play music composed by her, if available.

Catholic Family Album

Saint Hildegard von Bingen (1098–1179) worked to fulfill her dreams for her future in a time when society did not provide women with many opportunities. Hildegard worked hard to develop her great musical talent. She had an acute mind for science too and became a renowned botanist. She eventually joined a community of sisters who followed the Rule of Saint Dominic and was elected to be the leader of the community. Hildegard is a remarkable role model for women. Today her writings and music are an inspiration for others who seek to love God. In 2012, Pope Benedict XVI named her a Doctor of the Church.

Creating the Future You

Dreaming about your future can help you explore all of the possibilities life holds for you. Many of the world's creative geniuses have been great dreamers. Of course, in order to accomplish your goals, you will need to combine imagination with down-to-earth hard work. While your future begins with your dreams, you need to work with the grace of the Holy Spirit, with your family and with others to make those dreams become real, to become the person God calls you to be.

Here are some thought-provoking dream starters you can share in writing or with a friend:

1. How do I see myself after high school?
2. I am 25 years old. The newspaper is featuring an article about me. What does it say?
3. I am 35 years old and there is a high school reunion. What is my life like at 35?
4. I am 50 years old and I have just won the Lottery. What am I doing with the money?
5. I am 85 years old and at a family gathering celebrating my birthday. What makes me most proud? What do I want my family to remember about me?

66 Growing in Christ

Extending the Lesson

Using Activity Master 10B: Use the Activity Master "Signs Along the Way." This activity helps students evaluate specific situations and scenarios to see how they might respond to the challenges presented.

Self-Portraits: Make available art materials for students to draw a self-portrait of themselves as adults who have realized their eighth-grade dreams. They can incorporate signs, symbols or imagery that represents or points to some accomplishments they currently dream about that as an adult they would have fulfilled or achieved.

ONLINE ACTIVITIES FOR LESSON 10

Activity Master 10A

Name ....

Growth and Responsibility

Use this chart to recognize the growth and changes that have taken place in your life since infancy.

Infant's Growth	What's Happening with You Now
Physical Growth Growing quickly. Limited physical skills. Unable to care for own needs.	*Physical Growth*
Mental Growth Limited ability to learn. Directed by instinct, not reason.	*Mental Growth*
Emotional Growth Completely self-centered. Expects others to provide everything. Needs love and touching.	*Emotional Growth*
Spiritual Growth Experiences love and good things as coming from people, not God.	*Spiritual Growth*

Family Life Grade 8

Activity Master 10B

Name ....

Signs Along the Way

When you know what you're moving toward, it's easier to handle obstacles along the road. Remember, your major focus is to be the best you can be. Tell how you might handle these problems.

YIELD

You wanted to develop your art talent, so you saved your money for a long time and signed up for after-school lessons. Before you can begin, your mom breaks her leg. For several months, she'll need your help after school. What will you do? What will your attitude be?

____

____

NO U TURN

Your youth group volunteered to visit a convalescent home every Saturday, and it's taking up more time than you anticipated. Several people have dropped out, and you'd like to, also. What will you do? What will your attitude be toward the group and the convalescents?

____

____

DO NOT ENTER

You've finally made some friends at your new school. It feels terrific not to be a stranger anymore. Then one of the kids has a party at his house, and brings out some marijuana. What will you do and say? Are you willing to risk losing your new friends?

____

____

Family Life Grade 8

How to Find It How to Use It

Step 1: Click & Select

Go to RCLBFamilyLife.com
Click on the link for activities.
Then select the activity master you need.

Step 2: Print & Copy

Print each activity master in advance.
Then copy enough for everyone in the class.

Step 3: Share & Discuss

Once students have completed the activity, have them share and discuss their responses.

REVIEWING UNIT 5

Summary

- Ask the students to read through the Summary section.
- Invite them to ask questions about any points that are not clear to them.
- Make sure to expand on any points that were perhaps touched on only lightly during class time.

Thinking It Through

- Have students answer all three questions on the page.
- Assign each student a number from one through three.
- Have students share with the class their answer to the question that corresponds to their assigned number.

Matching It Up

Use this matching section to help the students identify the appropriate definition or description of a key concept, term or person from the unit.

REVIEWING UNIT 5

Name ....

Summary

Remember what you have learned in each of the lessons in God's Gift of Community.

LESSON 9: The Social Scene

- Peer pressure is a powerful influence upon our behavior that can work positively or negatively on the ways we make choices.
- God created us as social beings, or to live in community. Therefore, we need to experience a healthy sense of belonging within groups and community.
- Choosing those with whom we associate requires clear thinking and vigilance.

LESSON 10: Growing in Christ

- Life has meaning, and your life has a God-given purpose.
- In areas of your physical, mental, emotional, and spiritual life, you have specific responsibilities to mature in healthy and holy ways.
- Christian values guide you in attaining your dreams and finding happiness.

Thinking It Through

1. Which groups or communities have the most positive influences on your life?

2. How would you mentor, or what advice would you give to a sixth-grader toward achieving healthy and holy growth?

3. Why is it important to understand that your life has meaning and purpose?

Matching It Up

On each line, write the letter of the description in Column B that best goes with the term in Column A.

A	B
1. ...C... Commitment	A. To be relied upon
2. ...B... Emotional Responsibility	B. Listening to your feelings and to those of others
3. ...D... Mental Responsibility	C. Keeping your promises
4. ...E... Spiritual Responsibility	D. Learning as much as you can
5. ...A... Trust	E. Recognizing your dependence on God

Unit 5 Review 67

REVIEWING UNIT 5

Name..

Recalling Key Concepts

Circle the T if the statement is true. Circle the F if the statement is false.

1. Cliques are positive friendship groups that include other people. T (F)
2. God created human beings to live by themselves. T (F)
3. Gangs contribute positively to society by uniting people of good moral character. T (F)
4. Adolescence is a time of little maturing and a decrease in responsibilities. T (F)
5. Online social networking sites automatically provide a safe forum for everyone involved. T (F)

Fill in the missing words in these sentences.

6. Your ....**PURPOSE**.......... in life includes loving God according to his plan for you.
7. Having a sense of unity and belonging means being in ....**SOLIDARITY**... with others.
8. Future adult commitments in life include marriage, religious life, single life, or the ......**PRIESTHOOD**...... .
9. Good role models can help an individual work through their personal journey toward establishing their own..........**IDENTITY**........... .
10. Your faith, your ....**FAMILY**..........., and your good friends are the strongest sources of meaning in your life.

Working Together

In small groups, choose a Saint that is a role model for teens. Use reference books, the *Family Life* Web site and other Catholic Web sites and the Catholic Family Album feature in your book as sources of information. Write a report on the life of the Saint you choose. Be sure to include your reasons for selecting this particular person as your role model. Creatively present your report to the class and share it with your family.

68 Unit 5 Review

Teaching Tip

Note to Families: You may want to send a note to each family, thanking them for their help and support throughout the course of this program. Tell them how much you enjoyed working with them and learning from their children. Encourage families to continue talking with their children about the importance of family life and related issues.

REVIEWING UNIT 5

Recalling Key Concepts

- Use this section to help the students be able to accurately recall the key concepts from the unit.
- For the true and false section, you can have students correct any false statements.
- To help with the fill-in-the-blank section, you might want to provide a word bank on the board.

Working Together

- Choose a project that best fits the needs and abilities of your students, as well as your time schedule.
- Time permitting, have students complete the unit assessment individually or as a class; otherwise, encourage them to complete it at home.

Recalling Key Concepts

- Use this section to help the students be able to accurately remember key virtues presented this year from the unit.
- For the true and false section, you can have students correct any false statements.

Name ....

Recalling Key Concepts

Complete the sentence using one word from the word bank.

MODESTY	GENEROSITY	DIGNITY	SOLIDARITY	RESPECT

1. The **GENEROSITY** of my family and friends contributes to my happiness because of their sharing and my own.
2. Having **RESPECT** for yourself and others is a sign of maturity.
3. Living always with respect for the **DIGNITY** of the human person creates a consistent ethic of life.
4. The practice of **MODESTY** is one important way we learn to preserve our integrity in relationships.
5. Having a sense of unity and belonging means being in **SOLIDARITY** with others.

Circle the T if the statement is true. Circle the F if the statement is false.

1. Happiness is not based on a choice, but is something that just happens to you. T (F)
2. Some emotions are good, while others are bad. T (F)
3. Major threats to human life include only those that end human life. T (F)
4. Dating between teens is great practice for marriage. T (F)
5. Online social networking sites do have privacy and safety features that should be utilized. (T) F

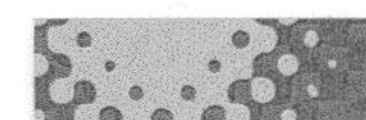

REVIEWING THIS YEAR

Name..

Matching It Up

On each line, write the letter of the description in Column B that best goes with the term in Column A.

A		B
1. ....A.... Basic Needs		A. Families provide food, shelter, security, and care.
2. ....E.... Commitment		B. I'm feeling angry, so I need to take a break.
3. ....D.... Contraception		C. The direct intentional killing of an innocent person
4. ....B.... Patience		D. A mentality and a practice contrary to God's plan for marriage
5. ....C.... Murder		E. Keeping your promises

Working Together

In groups, write a list of petitions for the whole class to offer in prayer as a way to contribute to the end of this year's learning.

REVIEWING THIS YEAR

Matching It Up

Use this matching section to help the students be able to identify the appropriate definition or description of a key concept, term or person from the unit.

Working Together

- Invite students to form small groups to write their petitions. Give each group time to get organized.
- Alternative projects are available online. Choose the project that best fits the need and abilities of your students, as well as your time schedule.

Summary

- Ask the students to read through the Summary section.
- Invite them to ask questions about any points that are not clear to them. Make sure to expand on any points that were perhaps touched on only lightly during class time.
- End the year in prayer using one from The Catholic Home section.

REVIEWING THIS YEAR

Name ....

Summary

We have learned about Family Life this year.

GOD'S GIFT OF FAMILY

- God has placed in the human heart the natural desire for happiness. The more we experience gratitude in life, the more we can come to know happiness.
- Feeling lost on our journey to happiness is a common emotion; but God has given us the gift of conscience to follow the right path to happiness.
- With an informed conscience and free will, we can choose to follow the right path to happiness.

GOD'S GIFT OF SELF

- Understanding your personality will help you have greater self-confidence and mature in your relationships with others.
- The Theological Virtue of hope opens up a person's heart to desire and expect the happiness God promises.
- Being able to face challenges in life with valor enables a person to turn problems into possibilities.

GOD'S GIFT OF LIFE

- Sin and moral evil are at the root of the many threats against human life.
- Scandal is behavior that leads another to sin. Showing respect for the dignity of the human person deters and prevents scandal.
- Abusive use of certain substances causes harm to a person, especially during adolescence.

GOD'S GIFT OF LOVE

- Developing and deepening friendships can be preparation for the lifelong commitment of marriage and parenting.
- Human sexuality is primarily concerned with our capacity to love and form relationships based on being male or female.
- Married love is to be self-giving and life-giving.

GOD'S GIFT OF COMMUNITY

- Choosing those with whom we associate requires clear thinking and vigilance.
- Life has meaning and a God-given purpose.
- Christian values guide us in attaining our dreams and finding happiness in life.

Grade 8 Review 71

Recognition of Achievement

The faith community of

____

proudly announces

____

and family have completed the eighth level of
RCL Benziger Family Life.

This young person has discovered:
God's gift of family
God's gift of self
God's gift of life
God's gift of love
God's gift of community

May every day provide you and your family new adventures in following Jesus and in living faithful Christian lives.

____
(Signed)

CUMULATIVE GLOSSARY

This glossary lists and defines the important terms as used in the context of the RCL Benziger *Family Life* program.

abortion: the direct and intentional killing of the human person before birth; direct abortion

abstinence: the avoidance of any sexual behavior or act

abuse: emotional, physical, sexual and/or verbal maltreatment of a person

acceptance: the act of approving or including another through words and actions

acne: pimples on the skin caused by oil clogged pores

addiction: a psychological dependence on something harmful; an unhealthy habit that is difficult to break

adolescence: a stage of life between childhood and adulthood; derived from the Latin, *adolescens*, meaning "growing toward"

adoption: a process where a person or couple legally and permanently care for a child who is not their biological child

adultery: the act of a married person engaging in sexual intercourse with someone who is not their spouse

affection: a feeling of fondness, tender attachment or sign of liking someone, being affected by a person or event

affirmation: the skill of acknowledging the importance of someone through honest praise, which encourages them to do their best

agape: see *charity*; the love of human beings for one another that comes from a love of God

alcohol: an addictive substance found in beer, wine and spirits/liquor

alcoholism: a disease involving a person's addiction to alcohol that harms the person and can result in harming others and often destroys relationships

almsgiving: sharing our blessings with people in need

altruism: the willingness to put the needs of others before one's own

annulment: a decree of nullity granted by the Church stating that the Sacrament of Marriage of a particular couple was invalid

anorexia: an eating disorder of habitually fasting and rigorous exercise based on an obsessive fear of being fat

assisted suicide: helping someone commit suicide

attitude: the ways someone looks at the world and relates to it

attraction: the sense of being drawn to or pulled toward something or someone; in relationships feelings of warmth, trust, care and generosity are experienced

bacteria: tiny, living organisms that can cause decay and other problems in the body

Baptism: Sacrament of Christian Initiation by which a person is joined to Christ, receives the gift of the Holy Spirit and becomes an adopted son or daughter of God the Father and member of the Church

birth order: the sequence of offspring and thus particular position within the family according to when the person was born

blended family: a family formed when adults with children from an earlier marriage enter a new marriage

body: the physical, mortal part of the person that together with the soul forms one unique human nature

budget: a financial tool to aid in managing money

bulimia: an eating disorder in which the person goes through cycles of binging and purging

capital punishment: the right of the government to execute convicted criminals

carbohydrates: a source of energy for the body found in breads, grains, cereals, pasta and rice

celibacy: the state of not being married

cell: the smallest unit of living things

character strength: a good habit that becomes a personal trait enabling one to live virtuously

charism: the grace of the Holy Spirit given to members of the Christian faithful to live out the Christian life in benefit to the Church

charity: the Theological Virtue of the love a person shows another because of one's love for God, who is the source of such love

chastity: the appropriate and successful integration of the gift of sexuality within the whole person in accord with their vocational state of life

chromosomes: threadlike structures inside each cell's nucleus that contain genes

circulatory system: the system that uses blood to deliver nutrients and oxygen to all parts of the body and pick up cells' waste products

cirrhosis: a disease of the liver that prevents it from removing harmful substances from the blood

civility: see *manners*; the character strength or practice of respectful, polite acts or expressions

cliques: social groups formed to exclude others, often resulting in the harassment of those excluded

common good: the sum total of social conditions which allows people, either as groups or as individuals, to reach their fulfillment more fully and more easily; it presupposes respect for the person

common sense: the ability to know what in general is good and then be able to apply that understanding to a specific situation in order to do the right thing

communication: an exchange of ideas, information, opinions or feelings

community: a group of living things that work together for a common purpose

compassion: the character strength of being able to identify with the situation and feelings of another, built on an attitude of equality

complementarity: to live with and for each other as equal in dignity, helping each other according to God's plan for the two genders

complementary sex: man and woman are not opposites, but complement each other because God created them to be one; also complementary gender

conception: the beginning of human life, the joining of egg and sperm to create new life

confidence: the strong feeling of certitude in oneself through accomplishment or a "can-do" attitude when faced with making a decision

conjugal love: see *spousal love*; the unique expression of sexual love between a husband and a wife who freely give their whole self to each other

conscience: the "inner voice" of a human being from God, within whose heart God's law is inscribed to discern or judge right from wrong, good from evil; a sense of obligation to do what is good and to avoid what is evil

consistent ethic of life: living always with respect for the dignity of the human person

contraception: the mentality and practice of separating the conjugal act from its two purposes of self-giving and life-giving

corporal: relating to or affecting the body

counsel: see *right judgment*; a Gift of the Holy Spirit in the ability to make right judgments, to choose what is right and good

courage: see *fortitude*; the strength to do or say what is right and good and to overcome fear, anxiety or any negative attitude that weakens one's confidence to do or say what is right and good

courtesy: a way of acting that shows respect for another person through words and deeds

culture: a way of life passed on through generations shaping people's beliefs, ideas, arts, customs, languages, diet and laws

curiosity: character trait of examining or wondering about someone or something

cyberbullying: the misuse of the Internet for the purposes of degrading or demeaning others

cytoplasm: the jelly-like fluid inside cells that contains the things a cell needs to live

delayed gratification: satisfaction of reaching an important goal after accepting discipline, sacrifice and inconveniences

dependability: trustworthy, can be relied on

dependence: relying on someone for help and support

depression: a physical or emotional illness that causes persistent sadness and interferes with rational thinking

dignity: inherent value of a human person instilled by God, who created people in his own image and likeness

diligence: in the context of sexual identity, the steadfast attention and appreciation of one's gender

discernment: prayerfully seeking to know God's will individually and personally so that the person's will can align with God's will

discipline: training that helps self-control

divorce: a legal procedure declaring the end of a civil marriage; different from an annulment in the Catholic Church

DNA: the basic ingredient of genes, containing the chemical code that enables genes to guide human growth; also called *deoxyribonucleic acid*

eating disorder: serious, unhealthy eating patterns, behavior or acts

ecology: the science or study of the relationships between living things and the environment

economics: the science or study of dealing with money

economy: the way in which the resources of a country or a community are managed

elderly: older adults, generally older than 70

embryo: the unborn child from the time of implantation in the womb up to the eighth week after conception

emotion: see *feeling*; a state of feeling or subjective experience of a person or event that results in physiological changes or inclines one to act or not act in regard to something felt or imagined to be good or evil

empathy: sensitivity to the needs and feelings of others

encyclical: a letter written by the Pope to be circulated throughout the Church in order to teach important truths at a given time

endangered: in danger of no longer existing, facing possible extinction

endocrine system: a collection of glands that make hormones to regulate body growth, reproductive development and metabolism

environment: the world in which people live, including every living and non-living thing

ethnicity: the particular customs, or ways of doing things, that are handed on from one generation to the next, connected with region, culture or religion

Eucharist: the Sacrament of the Body and Blood of Christ

eugenics: the manipulation of human mating and reproduction in order to "enhance" the human race by eliminating certain "undesirable" attributes

euthanasia: the deliberate killing of a person who is elderly, severely disabled or suffering from a serious or terminal illness

extended family: family that includes grandparents, aunts, uncles and cousins

family: two or more people related by blood, marriage or adoption

fecundity: openness to life; the capacity to generate new life

feeling: see *emotion*; a way of responding to something that has happened to the person, inclining one to act in a particular way

fertilization: see *conception*; the beginning of human life, the joining of egg and sperm to create new life

fetus: the developing unborn child from the third month after conception until birth

fidelity: being totally loyal to a person, also known as faithfulness

flowering plants: the largest plant group, including an amazing variety of trees, shrubs, vines, food plants, grasses and weeds

forgive: to reconcile with someone

forgiveness: the virtue of being able to offer acceptance and mercy by reconciling with the person who has caused harm or injury

fornication: sexual intercourse between an unmarried man and unmarried woman; a violation of the Sixth Commandment

fortitude: see *courage*; the Cardinal Virtue of courage or strength of mind and will to do what is good in the face of adversity or difficulty

foster care: the caring for a child who needs a family for a time

free will: the ability to recognize God as part of our lives and the power to choose between good and evil

gangs: social groups formed around criminal activity, often dealing with vandalism, drugs, robbery or murder

gender: the unique traits associated with being created male or female

generation: a group of related people born around the same time

generosity: the capacity, quality or activity of giving or sharing of oneself or what we have abundantly, beyond basic needs

generous: having an attitude that entails sharing talents, time and money with others

genetic: qualities of living things arising from a common origin and passed from generation to generation through reproduction

Gifts of the Holy Spirit: God-given powers and strengths that enable us to work toward the establishment of the Kingdom of God

Gospel: the Good News of God's mercy and love revealed in the life, Death and Resurrection of Christ

grace: the free and undeserved gift that God gives us to respond to our vocation to become his adopted children; the very life and love of God within us

gratification: having one's needs and or wants met; see *delayed gratification* or *instant gratification*

gratitude: the capacity and ability to choose to be appreciative of all that one receives

grooming: presenting a neat and clean physical appearance

guidance: the help and support people give to others in need

habit: something a person does over and over again, almost without having to think about it

habitat: the place where an animal survives

happiness: a state of contentment or gladness that we must choose to live found ultimately in the love of God

health: the working order of the person as God created and intended them to be; physical health relates to the body while spiritual health relates to the soul, but both are essential to the overall health of the person

CUMULATIVE GLOSSARY

Heaven: eternal life with God; being in the presence of God forever; communion of life and love with the Trinity and all the blessed; the state of supreme and definitive happiness, the goal of the deepest longing of humanity

heredity: refers to all traits and characteristics a person inherits from past generations

heterosexuality: sexual attraction to a person of the other or complementary sex

Holy Family: Jesus, Mary, and Joseph

homosexuality: sexual attraction to a person of the same sex

honesty: quality or character of being truthful with oneself, others and God

hope: the Theological Virtue by which a person desires and expects from God both happiness and the grace necessary to attain happiness

hormones: secretions that tell the body how to grow and how to use food; comes from the Greek word that means "to set in motion"

hospitality: accepting others for who they are by offering a welcoming environment

humility: the virtuous ability to be honest about oneself before God and respond to the needs of others when evident

hygiene: practice of cleanliness that promotes good health

identity: the sure knowledge of oneself

imagination: the ability to form a mental image of something that is not present or that does not exist; a gift from God that is a truly human power

implantation: five to seven days after conception, a fertilized ovum leaves the oviduct and attaches itself to the spongy, blood-rich lining of the uterus where it will be nourished until birth

income: money resources of a person, family or group

indissolubility: not able to be dissolved, the quality of permanence

individuality: the quality of being distinguished from others by the ability to think, wonder and choose; unique behavior

infertility: the inability to conceive a child

ingenuity: skills that are creative and used for the benefit of self and others

inspired: to be guided by the Holy Spirit

instant gratification: comforts, pleasures, wants and conveniences being met at the moment

instinct: the ability to carry out an action without having been taught

integrity: being true to the person God created one to be, seeking only what is true, beautiful and good about God, oneself, others and the world

intellect: the part of the mind that thinks, reasons and understands

interdependence: necessary cooperation

intimate: words, experiences or actions shared by those who are close to one another

intoxication: the diminishing effects on the physical or mental abilities to function normally; derived from a Latin word meaning "poisoned"

justice: the Cardinal Virtue of giving to another what is due to them, what is theirs by right, or ensuring that they have what they need

Kingdom of God: the reign or rule of God; God's saving power and love at work in us

laudableness: praiseworthiness, deserving of one's acknowledgment or reverence

life: the gift from God that allows us to move, grow, think and love

lifecycle: the period for each person from conception until natural death

love: to will the good of another

loyalty: supporting the people in one's life and caring about them

mammals: animals that nurse their young, are warm-blooded, have a backbone and have hair or fur all over their bodies

manners: see *propriety*; socially acceptable behaviors that help people function harmoniously as a community

marriage: a covenantal relationship between a man and a woman in which their spousal love is to be unitive and procreative; Sacrament in which a baptized man and a baptized woman promise love and faithfulness until death

married life: the joining of one man and one woman in the Sacrament of Marriage

mass media: communication intended for the public in various forms, such as print, audio, video and electronic media

maturity: the physical, intellectual, emotional and spiritual growth of the person through which one realizes their full potential appropriate to the person's intellectual or emotional level or age

maxim: a short saying that illustrates or teaches a certain value

mercy: loving kindness toward one who has caused offense in the context of forgiveness and compassion

mind: the part of a person that thinks, knows, learns, remembers and understands

moderation: enjoying things in a balanced and limited way

modesty: the virtue, or practice, of valuing, holding onto and guarding the sacredness of the human body through proper speech, attire and conduct

molestation: unwanted or inappropriate sexual contact

mood: a state of mind at a particular time that moves a person to some kind of action

morality: the goodness or evil of human acts

murder: the direct and intentional killing of an innocent person

muscular system: the system that allows bodily movement

nervous system: the control center of the human body

newborn: the stage in a person's life starting at birth and lasting for about a month

nicotine: an addictive substance that is inhaled in cigarette smoke

non-marital sex: any sexual activity outside the bonds of marriage

nucleus: the control center of a cell

nutrition: the study of foods and how the human body uses them

obedience: to follow willfully the direction, rule or guidance of another person

obligation: the action of committing oneself in service to or benefit for another

obstetrician: doctor specialized in prenatal care, childbirth and postnatal care

occasion of sin: situations that make it more difficult to do what is right and good

organ: body part that directs, or senses information

Original Sin: the first rejection of God's love, which had effects on all human beings

ovary: for plant life, the wide and round part located at the bottom of the pistil that contains seeds

oxygen: a clear, colorless, odorless, tasteless gaseous element produced by plants and needed by animals and people to live

parable: a short simple story told by Jesus to make a point

patience: waiting for something that one needs or wants when one is ready to receive it

peacemaker: one who encourages love and fosters understanding

pediatrician: doctor specialized in the development, care and treatment of children

peer pressure: influence of others upon a person, especially those close to the person, like one's friends

perseverance: the act of continuing with patient effort despite obstacles

personality: the sum total of all the traits and characteristics that express a person distinct from others

perspiration: the production and excretion of moisture from the sweat glands; increases during stress, cooling the body

philia: the affectionate bond of good friends

pistil: the vase-shaped part of a flower that contains the ovaries

pollen: dust-like substances of a flowering plant necessary for plants to reproduce

pollination: the process that prepares the flower to make new life

pornography: any effort to portray real or simulated sexual acts for use by others that betrays the truth and meaning of human sexuality and demeans persons as objects

poverty: a state of seriously lacking in resources or ability to obtain the basic necessities of life usually associated with monetary poverty

pray: the act of listening to and talking with God

pregnancy: nine-month period of development of a human being in the womb of the mother from conception to birth

prejudice: a preconceived adverse opinion or judgment of another

premarital sex: see *non-marital sex*; all sexual activity before marriage thereby violating the dignity of marriage

prenatal: caring for the mother and her child before birth

preteen: the age just before adolescence

pretentiousness: making unjustified or excessive demands, claims or giving greater value to something than warranted or deserved

procreation: participating with God in the creation of new life through sexual intercourse or marital love

profit: the amount of money left over after all the expenses have been subtracted from the income

promise: a solemn vow

propriety: see *civility*; knowing how to be respectful in speech and conduct; good manners

prostitution: the performance of sexual acts for money violating the dignity of the human person

protein: a nutrient found in fish, fowl, meat and beans

prudence: the Cardinal Virtue of knowing what is right and consistently making good judgments so to choose the correct means to accomplish it

psychology: the science and study of mental and behavioral patterns of the individual that helps one to understand how people relate to others and their environment

puberty: the period of rapid growth associated with the development of the reproductive system

purity of heart: the desire to do the will of God, especially in the areas of charity, chastity and faith

racism: the belief that people are superior or inferior because of their race

rape: forced violent sexual intercourse violating the dignity of the human person

Reconciliation: the Sacrament that welcomes us back to close friendship with God and people; also referred to as the Sacrament of Penance and Reconciliation

recycling: a process that reclaims discarded paper, plastic, glass, aluminum and other metals so they can be used again

reproduce: the ability to produce or make new life of the same kind

reproductive system: the system that allows a male and female to have offspring

resilience: the ability to adjust or to change with courage in order to deal with failure; being able to bounce back and move ahead in life

respect: positive regard or esteem; a sign and attitude that values the person as important; honoring the inherent dignity of a person because of their sacredness

respiratory system: the system that allows the body to breathe air in and out, inhaling oxygen and exhaling carbon dioxide

responsibility: the quality of being dependable or accountable for one's attitude, decisions and actions by putting the care for self, others and the world around us into action

reverence: showing honor or respect for the sacredness of human life by cherishing life as a gift and caring for life as being precious

right judgment: see *counsel*; a Gift of the Holy Spirit that helps a person make good moral decisions

role model: a person whose attributes or behavior is imitated by another

Sacrament: an efficacious sign of grace, given to the Church by Christ, by which God shares his life and love with us

sacred: identified as holy and close to God

sacredness: the setting aside as holy thereby becoming closer to God

sacrifice: giving up something for the good of self or another

scandal: behavior that leads another to do evil

seed: the product of pollination that contains a protective hard coat or skin that surrounds the inner core of cells that will develop into a plant

self-acceptance: the ability to discover, appreciate and value yourself as God created you

self-control: restraining from impulses, selfishness and sin

self-esteem: having confidence and satisfaction in oneself

self-giving love: being unselfish with our time, talent and treasure through the giving of ourselves for another's benefit

senses: the five senses or abilities of sight, hearing, touch, taste and smell that enables a person to experience the physical world and to learn

separation: time apart spent by a husband and wife to work out their problems

sexual abuse: unwanted and uninvited sexual activity that is physically or emotionally imposed or forced upon another person

sexual attraction: attraction to another person based on their gender; part of God's plan to help a man and a woman become husband and wife

sexual identity: see *sexuality*; everything about a person related to their gender

sexual intercourse: see *spousal love*; the physical act of love showing a full commitment proper between spouses as gifts to one another

sexuality: that aspect of human nature concerned with the capacity to love and form relationships based on the person being created either male or female

sin: a deliberate thought, word, deed or omission contrary to God's law

social evil: the impact of personal sin that influences or includes the sins of others

social involvement: a person's participation in the life of a community

social networking: in the context of online practice, a phenomenon where people are increasingly forming social groups or friends via online forums

social sin: the effect of sin, over time, which can affect society and its institutions to create "structures of sin"

society: a group of persons brought together organically by a principle of unity that goes beyond each one of them; the good of each person is the purpose of society and all social institutions

solidarity: a sense of unity and belonging with another or within a group of people

somatotropin: the "growth hormone" released by the pituitary gland in the brain

soul: the spiritual immortal part of the human person, immediately created by God, which is separated from the body at death and with which it will be reunited in the final resurrection

spiritedness: a feeling of excitement or energy that boosts a sense of courage within a person

spiritual: relating to or affecting the spirit or soul of a person

spousal love: see *conjugal love*; the unique expression of love between a husband and a wife who freely give their whole self to each other; marital love

spouse: a husband (male) or a wife (female)

stamen: in flowers, the rods on which pollen is kept

stem: part of a plant that holds up the plant and carries water from the roots to the leaves, flowers and fruit

stepparent: a parent through a remarriage who is not the biological parent

stereotype: erroneous ideas or false preconceived notions about an individual

steward: one who uses the gift of God's creation and its resources with responsibility and care

stewardship: the actions of responsibly caring for what God has given in service to others

suicide: the taking of one's own life; a violation of the dignity of the human person

teenage: see *adolescence*; the time a person is between the ages of 13 and 18

temperance: the Cardinal Virtue that moderates the attraction of pleasure or a person's actions so that the person does what is right

temptation: an attraction either from outside oneself or from within to act contrary to right reason and the Commandments of God

tenacity: being persistent and faithful in maintaining oneself the way God created that person to be

terrorism: violent acts for the sole purpose of causing intense violent fear upon a person or group of people

thankfulness: being glad and grateful

thoughtfulness: considering the needs of another by putting oneself in their place

tithing: the giving back to God one's time, talent and treasure to support the Church

trust: to know that a person cares about you

valor: the virtuous ability to face challenges in life with the strength of mind, will and spirit

values: those things believed to be important to living a moral and holy life; derived from the Latin, *valēre*, meaning "to be of worth"

vigilance: an attitude and skill of being alert and watchful of a person's surroundings and interaction with others

violence: acts with force in which harm, injury, damage or death could or does occur

virtue: a habit of acting according to what is moral and good

virus: a tiny form of germs that causes disease

vocation: a call from God to a particular way of life in service to others, which in turn honors God: single, married, ordained or consecrated; the universal call to holiness

war: armed conflict between nations or organized groups of peoples

wellness: soundness of mind, body and spirit; healthy living

wisdom: see *prudence*; knowing what is right and consistently making good judgments so to choose the correct means to accomplish it

Works of Mercy: virtuous actions that help others in need, grouped as Corporal (bodily needs) and Spiritual (spiritual needs)

young adult: a person between the ages of 19 and 30

zygote: the initial stage of a cell formed by the union of a sperm and an egg containing the complete genetic plan for new life